WHAT YOUR COLLEAGUES ARE SAYING

The book is a great resource and provides a deep dive into culturally responsive and relevant mathematics practices. It includes rich examples and tasks that can be used during instruction, professional development, and research initiatives in mathematics education that seek to embrace culture and emphasize the relevance of mathematics in our everyday lives. Notably, the culturally relevant mathematics task-building framework provides clear guidance for creating cognitively demanding tasks that draw on the knowledge and experiences of individuals' communities and empower them to address existing inequities.

Ruthmae Sears
Associate Professor in Mathematics Education
University of South Florida
Tampa, FL

This phenomenal book provides practical approaches to analyze, identify, and create culturally relevant mathematics tasks that help secondary mathematics teachers create opportunities to connect to students' lived experiences.

Lateefah Id-Deen
Associate Professor of Mathematics Education
Kennesaw State University
Kennesaw, GA

Thank you, Matthews, Jones, and Parker, for the secondary version of *Engaging in Culturally Relevant Math Tasks*. You provide secondary teachers with the tools to deepen their understanding of culturally relevant pedagogy for the classroom. Our students need it!

John Staley
Past President NCSM, Mathematics Education Leadership
Past Chair U.S. National Commission on Mathematics Instruction
Baltimore County Public Schools
Randallstown, MD

The authors of *Engaging in Culturally Relevant Math Tasks* have provided a well-needed modern vision of what mathematics teaching and learning at the secondary level should look like in the 21st century. Teachers who read this book will be given the tools to begin developing rich, engaging, meaningful mathematics experiences that foster joy and creativity for their students while empowering students and teachers as change agents.

Robin Wilson
Professor, Department of Mathematics
Loyola Marymount University
Los Angeles, CA

In this much-needed work, Matthews, Jones, and Parker build seamlessly on their prior volume for Grade K–5 teachers. The authors provide practical guidance to support teachers in finding, adapting, or creating tasks with challenging contexts that help develop students' hope, empathy, and agency. This is an invaluable resource for teachers who want to center students' voices and lived experiences.

For those who fear that culturally relevant math can be misconstrued as formulaic tricks or bombastic rhetoric, this book lives up to the title's promise of fostering hope. Readers will find a wealth of frameworks for reaching students where they are at, for illuminating the cultural landscapes that escape our notice, and for inspiring students to see how mathematical ways of knowing and social motivations for inquiry can be united with rigor, compassion, and scholarly excellence.

The authors remind us that quality math tasks are not solely defined by their level of cognitive demand but must also give deliberate attention to inquiring about and centering the cultural brilliance and wisdom of students and their communities. This book is a must-read for middle and high school math teachers.

What a wonderful resource full of concrete, actionable strategies for creating more inclusive, culturally responsive mathematics classrooms. The authors offer not only a multitude of rich task examples that are classroom tested, but they also provide guidance for designing mathematically meaningful tasks that are relevant for the students and communities you serve. At the heart of their work is a deep respect for students' identities and abilities and for the work of teachers committed to a more just, equitable, and hopeful approach to mathematics education.

Engaging in Culturally Relevant Math Tasks

Engaging in Culturally Relevant Math Tasks

Fostering Hope in the Middle and High School Classroom

Lou Edward Matthews

Shelly M. Jones

Yolanda A. Parker

For information:

Corwin
A SAGE Company
2455 Teller Road
Thousand Oaks, California 91320
(800) 233–9936
www.corwin.com

SAGE Publications Ltd.
1 Oliver's Yard
55 City Road
London, EC1Y 1SP
United Kingdom

SAGE Publications India Pvt. Ltd.
B 1/I 1 Mohan Cooperative
Industrial Area
Mathura Road, New Delhi 110 044
India

SAGE Publications Asia-
Pacific Pte. Ltd.
18 Cross Street #10–10/11/12
China Square Central
Singapore 048423

President: Mike Soules
Vice President and Editorial Director:
  Monica Eckman
Publisher: Erin Null
Content Development Editor:
  Jessica Vidal
Editorial Assistant: Nyle De Leon
Production Editor: Tori Mirsadjadi
Copy Editor: Amy Hanquist Harris
Typesetter: Integra
Proofreader: Scott Oney
Indexer: Integra
Cover Designer: Gail Buschman
Marketing Manager:
  Margaret O'Connor

MIX
Paper from
responsible sources
FSC® C103567

This book is printed on acid-free paper.

22 23 24 25 26 10 9 8 7 6 5 4 3 2 1

Contents

To access online resources for this book, visit the *Engaging With Culturally Relevant Math Tasks (Secondary)* Free Resources tab on the Corwin website or visit **https://bit.ly/3LHcx88**.

Preface

I understand the importance of this work and have no problem with completing this assignment. But I don't know how I will be able to implement this in the classroom at my school. I don't know how it will be received.

—Joyce, a secondary teacher

This was part of a reflection from a graduate student in one of our mathematics education courses. The students, all teachers, were asked to complete an assignment incorporating culturally relevant teaching into a lesson plan. The concern expressed in the reflection was about potential pushback associated with delivering such a lesson—not from students, but from administrators and possibly parents.

Over the years, we have encountered many Joyces on our journey. We wanted to write a book to help fundamentally shift the way middle school and secondary teachers like Joyce create experiences of hope and engagement in mathematics. Every day, everywhere, teachers plan and design mathematics lessons based on the curriculum they have, their knowledge of students, and, of course, their own experiences. We see important opportunities in every mathematics classroom to shape how young people experience mathematics and the world around them. Today's students face adversity unlike anything previous generations of young people have seen. In addition to the social and family challenges that teens and young adults "normally" face, they must navigate through the effects of social media and maintain their mental well-being in the face of added pressures such as racial and social injustice, environmental climate change, and the coronavirus pandemic. These students will soon be adults and will need tools to learn how to effectively manage what they will encounter in the world, and we believe in the power of mathematics to help them do just that. They can deepen their understandings of themselves while they do math to fight for justice, leverage their voice, and advocate for themselves.

As authors, our experiences run the span of K–12 and teacher education in the United States, the Caribbean, South America, and Africa. Together, the three of us bring a combined experience of over 75 years as classroom teachers, teacher preparation leaders, teacher leaders, researchers, and system leaders. In this book, we aim to open up our practice and share our insight so that you and your students may reimagine math, the world, your communities, and yourselves in these experiences.

WHAT THIS BOOK IS ABOUT

Among the things that influence students' learning experiences are the quality of mathematics tasks in which they engage, the discourse those tasks support, and the interactions they foster. Culturally relevant mathematics engages and empowers students, helping them make connections to themselves, their communities, and the world around them. We believe that planning and implementing culturally relevant mathematical tasks provides one of the greatest opportunities to inspire and impact student learning in mathematics. Teachers can affirm the greatness in students while connecting to their community.

> *Culturally relevant mathematics engages and empowers students, helping them make connections to themselves, their communities, and the world around them.*

This book is designed as a primary resource for educators engaging in mathematics task adoption, design, planning, and implementation in ways that have potential to engage, inspire, and empower students in grades 6–12. Our goal is to offer a practical and inspirational approach to culturally relevant mathematics instruction in the form of intensive, in-the-moment guidance and practical classroom tools to meet teachers where they are and help grow their practice day by day. We focus on research-based and learner-centered teaching practices to help students develop deep conceptual understanding, procedural knowledge and fluency, and application in all mathematical content in grades 6–12.

WHO THIS BOOK IS FOR

This book is designed for the professional development of middle and high school teachers—both those who are established and those early in their career. It's also designed for mathematics teacher educators, mathematics teacher leaders and mentors, coaches and instructors in clinical residency programs, curriculum designers, principals, and consultants who teach and design professional learning experiences in 6–12 mathematics. Those teaching and learning in teacher preparation programs will see this as a useful anchor text in mathematics methods and pedagogy coursework. This book will be especially beneficial for teachers whose students are culturally different from them and who want to teach mathematics in more authentic, inclusive, and meaningful ways.

HOW THIS BOOK WORKS

We see teachers as *engineers* who can design and refine engaging and inspiring mathematics learning experiences driven by the kind of high-quality and culturally relevant mathematics tasks that will empower and engage students. We have written this to be interactive and applicable, providing practice-guided knowledge that preservice, novice, and veteran teachers can use to shape culturally relevant experiences for all students while systematically building lessons that are standards-based. We used the following elements of the engineering design process—*ask, imagine, plan, create,* and *improve*—to drive interactive teacher moments within each chapter throughout the book (see Figure 0.1).

FIGURE 0.1 ● Engineering design of culturally relevant mathematics tasks

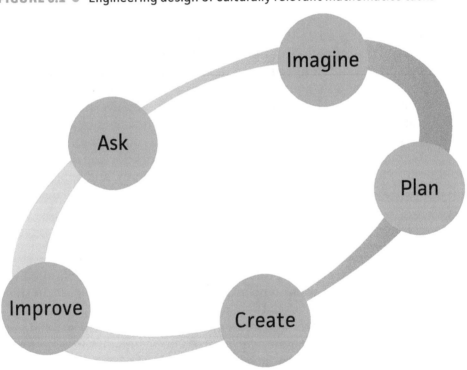

In *ask*, teachers consider the important and essential problems and the constraint of teaching. Teachers have opportunities to *imagine* what culturally relevant mathematics tasks would look, sound, and feel like. With a solid understanding of what culturally relevant math tasks are, teachers work to *plan* high-quality mathematics tasks and *create*, design, and adapt culturally relevant mathematics tasks and experiences. Teachers work continuously to *improve* on the process of task creation as they incorporate quality tasks into lesson implementation and refinement.

This book serves as a pathway for moving through this process, offering tools, examples, and milestones along the way. As such, the engineering design process is used to structure the book in two ways: (1) as an organizing feature of the chapters to signify the major focus of content and major sections, and (2) to frame the key experiences for teachers as they move through the content of the book. By this, we mean that chapters provide teachers with practical guidelines for creating and refining mathematical tasks and lessons through the lens of culturally relevant instruction, they offer opportunities to rehearse approaches for implementation, and they guide teachers in reflection for further growth.

We share vignettes throughout the book as a way to illustrate what culturally responsive mathememathics tasks and experiences look like in action. All names used in the vignette boxes throughout are pseudonyms.

In addition to opportunities for reflection throughout the chapters, you will also find a summary and list of discussion questions at the end of each chapter. Please take time to pause and think through each of the questions, making a specific commitment to what is presented in the chapter through your responses. Our work in this book is based on research and has been honed by our years of working with teachers in a variety of settings. Theoretically, this book is grounded in the research on culturally relevant pedagogy (CRP). At the core of the content of the book is the culturally relevant cognitively demanding (CRCD) rubric in Chapter 3.

While mathematics teaching consists of a wide range of teacher activities, this book focuses unapologetically on mathematics tasks. This is intentional. We see tasks as possible points of liberatory action in mathematics, and we hope this book serves as a useful guide and resource on your journey of empowering your students through culturally relevant mathematics teaching.

Acknowledgments

I want to acknowledge God, family, the network of Black math educators, and math creators too numerous to mention who held space and time over the years to "write this vision."

—Lou Edward Matthews

I would like to thank all the students and teachers whom I have learned from over my 30 years as an educator. A special thanks to those students and teachers whose stories are featured in this book, including Ashley, Beatriz, Brittany, Courtney, Deborah, Evan, George, Julie, Katie, and Rayna. Much gratitude to my colleagues Michelle and Gina and to the Math Teachers' Circle 4 Social Justice (MTC4SJ) in Connecticut. I give honor to God and extend a heartfelt hug to my family and friends for their unwavering support.

—Shelly M. Jones

I want to thank God for this opportunity, which I do not take lightly; my family for their endless love and support; my students for always challenging me to improve as a teacher; and my colleagues for being the iron that sharpens iron (Proverbs 27:17).

—Yolanda A. Parker

PUBLISHER'S ACKNOWLEDGMENTS

Corwin gratefully acknowledges the contributions of the following reviewers:

Michelle D. McKnight
K–5 Mathematics Instructional Coach
South Windsor Public Schools

Georgina Rivera
Administrator
Bristol Public Schools

Ishmael Robinson
K–12 Math Supervisor
Saint Paul Public Schools

Kaneka Turner
Elementary Math Specialist
ReImage Mathematics

About the Authors

Source: Lou Matthews

Lou Edward Matthews, PhD, is a global mathematics creative and founder of InspireMath, which is committed to building inspiring, sustainable mathematics platforms and culturally relevant education experiences in communities around the world. As Director of Mathematics and Science at Urban Teachers, a national teacher residency program with Johns Hopkins University and American University, Dr. Lou supports the recruitment, coaching, and deployment of culturally competent mathematics teachers and the work of professors and coaches in Baltimore, Washington, D.C., Philadelphia, and Dallas. Dr. Lou has served the mathematics community as a leading equity and racial justice advocate, speaker, and scholar over the last 25 years. He has authored studies, book chapters, blogs, and videos on culturally relevant mathematics teaching, including contributing to the book *The Brilliance of Black Children in Mathematics: Beyond the Numbers and Toward a New Discourse.* Dr. Lou also created the *Hope Wheel©* and the *Culturally Relevant Cognitively Demanding (CRCD) Mathematics Task Rubric.* In response to the global crisis of racial injustice and the COVID-19 pandemic, Dr. Lou pioneered learning spaces like *Hope Wheel©* and *Pi Before Dinner,* a virtual space and media channel for amplifying and illuminating the voices and images of Black children, families, and community in mathematics.

Source: Dominick Daniels
Photography

Shelly M. Jones, PhD, is a professor of mathematics education at Central Connecticut State University (CCSU). She teaches undergraduate mathematics content and methods courses for preservice teachers as well as graduate-level mathematics content, curriculum, and STEM (science, technology, engineering, and mathematics) courses for in-service teachers. Before joining the CCSU faculty, Jones was a middle school mathematics teacher and a K–12 mathematics supervisor. She provides mathematics professional development nationally and internationally. She has been an educator for 30 years. She serves her community by working with various professional and community organizations. You can see her CCSU TEDx talk on YouTube, where she talks about culturally relevant mathematics. She is a contributing author for the book *The Brilliance of Black Children in Mathematics: Beyond the Numbers and Toward a New Discourse* and the author of *Women Who Count: Honoring African American Women Mathematicians.* Jones's accomplishments have earned her recognition by the *Mathematically Gifted & Black* website as a Black History Month 2019 Honoree.

Source: Glen E. Ellman

Yolanda A. Parker, PhD, has been an educator for more than 25 years and has been full-time faculty at Tarrant County College (TCC)–South Campus for more than 10 years in the mathematics department, where she primarily teaches statistics and mathematics for teachers courses. She has a BS in applied math from Texas A&M University in College Station, Texas; MA in liberal studies from Dartmouth College in Hanover, New Hampshire; and PhD in mathematics education from Illinois State University in Normal, Illinois. She was honored as one of the 2017 Hidden Figures of Dallas: Top Women of Color in STEM by the National Society of Black Engineers, Dallas/Fort Worth Professionals chapter, and has been featured in *Women Who Count: Honoring African American Women Mathematicians*. She was also recognized as the campus recipient of the 2017 TCC Chancellor's Award for Exemplary Teaching, the highest award a TCC faculty can receive. Her research interests include the effectiveness of mathematics manipulatives with adult learners, algebra teacher self-efficacy, and culturally relevant, cognitively demanding mathematics tasks.

PART I

Imagining Culturally Relevant Mathematics Teaching

In Chapters 1 through 3, we set a vision for culturally relevant mathematics task design by exploring shifts in mathematics teaching and learning along with key features of culturally relevant mathematics practices, teaching, and tasks.

CHAPTER 1

What Is Culturally Relevant Mathematics Teaching?

In this chapter, we will

- Identify four shifts in drivers for mathematics teaching and learning at the secondary level
- Distinguish between traditional and reform expectations for classroom practice and how they shape the teacher's role
- Explore the basic tenets of culturally relevant mathematics teaching (CRMT)

MODERN EXPECTATIONS FOR MATHEMATICS

Modern expectations for mathematics teaching and learning (which we'll broadly refer to in this book with the term "math reform") are undergoing rapid change. This generation of adolescents will be known as the most racially, linguistically, and ethnically diverse and more digitally exposed than any previous generation. This dynamic feature of the classroom has pushed us to rethink several essential questions about teaching and learning math:

1. How should learners experience mathematics concepts and ideas?
2. How should we teach mathematics dynamically?

3. How can we harness rich cultural and ethnic diversity for powerful mathematics experiences?

4. What are the purposes of learning mathematics?

In this chapter, we will explore each of these questions by examining the four drivers:

1. Shifts in Mathematics Learning
2. Shifts in Teacher Roles
3. Shifts in Mathematics Content
4. Shifts in Making Mathematics Matter

DRIVER 1:
SHIFTS IN MATHEMATICS LEARNING

The most significant driver of math reform in the last two decades is a change in what students experience when they actually "do" math. This change moves away from a reliance on simply learning isolated procedures and toward a more active student presence in making meaning. Traditionally, classroom experiences may have consisted of students learning key vocabulary, watching the teacher do guided examples, and then engaging in a lot of independent practice. The singular goal of this script was getting correct answers to prescribed problems.

By contrast, most math reform curricula support classrooms in which students are challenged to use a variety of problem-solving strategies and where they connect, communicate, collaborate, and grow their ideas. For example, the Common Core State Standards (CCSS) for Mathematical Practice describe a set of eight *practices* (see Figure 1.1) that feature active student math learning across grades K–12.

FIGURE 1.1 ● Common Core State Standards for Mathematical Practice

Math Practice 1	Make sense of problems and persevere in solving them.
Math Practice 2	Reason abstractly and quantitatively.
Math Practice 3	Construct viable arguments and critique the reasoning of others.
Math Practice 4	Model with mathematics.
Math Practice 5	Use appropriate tools strategically.
Math Practice 6	Attend to precision.
Math Practice 7	Look for and make use of structure.
Math Practice 8	Look for and express regularity in repeated reasoning.

What do you notice as you look at the practices? If you learned math in the last several decades in the United States, Canada, or some other Western nation, there are probably many features that stand out as markedly different from the math you likely experienced growing up. For one, in the very first practice, students are asked to "make sense" of problems and "persevere" in the process. This calls for students having greater awareness of the problem-solving process (a kind of mindfulness, really) as they work problems. The emphasis on persevering is also a focus on student effort and mindfulness as key to problem-solving.

For example, think about the student who is asked to calculate the percentage change in population for Austin, Texas, from 2016 with a population of 908,000 people to 2020 with 962,000 people. The student mistakenly uses a formula they learned and says, "a negative 5% change." When pushed to consider if this is reasonable, the student realizes that there is no way to get a negative change when the population actually increases. Upon reflection, the student reconsiders their response based on their sense making. The student is asked to check the reasonableness of the solution as opposed to the teacher pointing it out. We love this because it represents a certain attention to strategies and thinking in a way that shifts ownership away from the teacher and onto the student.

One hopeful consequence of students taking this ownership is that they can begin to see themselves as problem solvers. We also imagine, and discuss throughout this book, that they might also see themselves as problem *creators*. This has the potential for students to enjoy the potential richness of doing math problems they relate to and enjoy.

The practices also emphasize using the "precision" (see Math Practice 6) of tools and symbols. Yet there is a very deliberate attempt throughout the practices to strike a balance between fluency with procedures and language and interpreting situations in real life. For instance, students are asked to interpret situations mathematically as they "model" (Math Practice 4) and "look for" patterns and "structure" (Math Practice 7). In each of the practices, we appreciate the opportunities students have to do and create through the mathematics process. Throughout the book, we deliberately extend this creativity into the realm of mathematizing students' lived experiences as a way of engaging in math practice.

ASK

Think about your own experiences in middle school or high school mathematics. In what ways did you experience the math practices listed in Figure 1.1?

DRIVER 2: SHIFTS IN TEACHER ROLES

The focus on active student sense making requires new thinking for the role of the teacher. In response, the National Council of Teachers of Mathematics (NCTM, 2014) has advocated teachers shift from being deliverers of mathematical knowledge to playing more dynamic roles of facilitators, guides, and co-constructors of mathematical knowledge. This requires teachers to create lessons that use robust and challenging math tasks that allow students to grapple with important mathematics ideas. Compare that with a more traditional approach where mathematics is seen as static information presented by the teacher, and students memorize procedures to solve routine problems.

As facilitators, teachers encourage students to share their thinking, refine their strategies, and generate new knowledge. Here, mathematics is not taught as isolated facts and procedures but explored through multiple pathways while making connections to other concepts. For example, imagine a word problem in which students can figure out for themselves that solving a linear function is a possible solution strategy, rather than being told that this is the tool they should use.

Teachers also create meaningful interactions where students learn through collaboration with others in their math community. So even as students are encouraged to utilize a variety of approaches, teachers create spaces and opportunities for them to communicate their constructed ideas and then support them in the meaning making. A comparison of traditional teacher approaches and reform expectations is depicted in Figure 1.2.

FIGURE 1.2 ● A comparison of traditional views and reform expectations of mathematics teaching

TRADITIONAL VIEWS	REFORM EXPECTATIONS
Mathematics as information to be memorized or applied with correct procedures	Mathematics as dynamic sense making
Teachers as explainers of information	Teachers facilitate rich tasks, discourse, and interactions
Students learn through drill and practice	Students as mathematics meaning makers

Version A

Solve the proportion $\dfrac{4}{18} = \dfrac{10}{x}$

Version B

Freda makes $8.50 for every $10 her brother makes. If Freda makes $340 this week, how much does her brother make? Solve using a proportion.

ASK

How do the following two tasks reflect differences in reform and traditional expectations?

In Version A, and with traditional teaching, students might be led to use cross products or equivalent fraction strategies to solve for *x*, but they might be uncertain *why* they need to find the proportion. This process is listed in the traditional views column as "Students learn through drill and practice" and "Teacher as explainer of information." With Version B, the teacher might have students use their own strategies for finding the brother's weekly earnings. Students would then discuss the problem with classmates to hear other strategies. The teacher would make connections between strategies and with previous learning of equivalent fractions, making the connection that a proportion is two equivalent ratios. This follows the reform expectation of "Teachers facilitate rich tasks, discourse, and interactions." Furthermore, students might be interested to learn that in 2020 the pay gap between women and men still persisted and women earned about 85% of what men earned based on median hourly earnings. The context of the wage gap provides "meaning" to the mathematics. When students find the solution, they would be using math to "make sense" of the problem.

In strict terms, the traditional and reform approaches represent shifting—even polarizing—expectations for the work of teachers, as well as for the experiences of math doers. Adjusting to these shifting expectations can be challenging for teachers because they are often forced to characterize their current teaching practices as "good" or "bad." We move past calling this way or that way right or wrong to thinking of the shift along a continuum of student ownership and agency. Competent, effective teaching requires us to understand these shifts.

DRIVER 3: SHIFTS IN MATHEMATICS CONTENT

Over the last 75 years, there have been several periods of shift in organizing the content of mathematics curriculum. Most recently, in their publication series *Catalyzing Change in Middle School Mathematics* (2020) and *Catalyzing Change in High School Mathematics: Initiating Critical Conversations* (2018), one of NCTM's key recommendations was to broaden the purposes of learning mathematics in order to create high-quality secondary mathematics programs. In such programs, students would develop deep mathematical understandings of the essential math concepts. Currently, far too many of our students experience mathematics instruction that is focused on learning skills and procedures without connections to themselves, their families, or their communities. By making connections to students' lived experiences, we can better engage and motivate them because we are connecting mathematics to something they are familiar with and something they care about.

While it is important for schools and school districts to identify a list of content domains for middle school teachers to address (i.e., number, ratio and proportion, statistics and probability, geometry and measurement), it is even more important *how* teachers help students develop these deep understandings of the mathematics. At the high school level, *Catalyzing Change* recommends trimming down the amount of content covered so that students can "learn and understand foundational mathematics at a deep level" (2018, p. 5). They propose a set of essential concepts from number, algebra, statistics and probability, and geometry and measurement. Increasingly, our everyday lives are driven by data; hence, it is imperative that students receive a mathematics education that prepares them to be mathematically and statistically literate members of society.

In the reimagined mathematics programs described earlier, educators would plan mathematics experiences where students could understand and critique the world around them using mathematics. This is another way to broaden the purpose of mathematics learning, and it is aligned with one of the goals of culturally relevant pedagogy that you will read more about in Chapter 3. As adolescents and soon-to-be young adults, middle and high school students need to be able to critically examine the world and to make informed decisions that impact themselves, their families, and their communities. They will need mathematical and statistical tools to understand social and political issues they are confronted with.

Another reason to broaden the purpose of mathematics learning, and maybe the most critical in turning around the current system that is failing many of our youth, is to reimagine the mathematics classroom as a space where all students can experience the wonder, joy, and beauty of mathematics. When we get to know our students and honor what they bring to the classroom, we can create this space for them. We build trust with them, and they see meaning in the mathematics they engage in. Throughout this book, you will read how this purpose will undoubtedly lead to mathematics that is cultural in nature.

DRIVER 4: SHIFTS IN MAKING MATHEMATICS MEANINGFUL

In one of our early experiences supporting the teaching of mathematics, Lou conducted a series of workshops called *Making Mathematics Meaningful* with a handful of elementary and middle school teachers in Bermuda in 2001. The phrase itself represents a fourth driver of what we want to see in modern mathematics classrooms. It is easily the most sensitive and aspirational element: harnessing the power of mathematics in engaging communities of doers. As mentioned before, students entering today's classrooms will be the most racially, linguistically, and ethnically diverse of any previous generation. Yet mathematics has a long history of exclusion when it comes to *what counts* as mathematics, *who* can do mathematics, and *who* has access to engaging mathematics.

Mathematics has a long history of exclusion when it comes to what counts as mathematics, who can do mathematics, and who has access to engaging mathematics.

Much of what students have seen honored as the work of mathematicians is presented as white and male. Recently, however, developments in accounting for the history of mathematics reveal powerful insights into the non-European origins of mathematics. The reality of mathematical development is that all cultures have played significant roles in its contribution (Joseph, 2011). In fact, most, if not all, of school mathematics has had some origin outside of European thought. For example, the

Ishango bone uncovered in central Africa has notches that show doubling, prime numbers, and patterns of numbers based on 10. It is dated to approximately 20,000 BCE. Another ancient civilization, the Maya of what is now Mexico and Central America, are known for using the first symbol for zero. It is heartbreaking that students don't always see themselves as mathematicians. Exposing them to mathematics' "hidden figures"—Black, Indigenous, and People of Color (BIPOC)—is a powerful message that mathematics is the domain of everyone. Being able to connect who they are to who they see doing mathematics is critical to having children experience mathematics with joy and wonder. It is also helpful in increasing the diversity of math and STEM-related jobs and occupations.

We think it is important for teachers to radically rethink how culture and community can complement and challenge teaching. Seeing math identity as cultural and ethnic identity holds great promise in the new mathematics classroom itself. This is challenging for us because math has been taught through a color-blind lens—that is, as a subject that is "pure" and culturally neutral. When teachers say math is neutral and "1 + 1 = 2 everywhere," they often rob themselves of understanding the contributions of others or of exploring new ways of thinking about mathematics. This position shows up in what comprises much of the work students do in what we call "naked math." This is where students see doing math as simply calculating answers using symbols and procedures without much regard to "why." This position has been harmful to all students.

Math as sense making provides opportunities for students to make meaning of things that matter to them.

Math as sense making provides opportunities for students to make meaning of things that matter to them. The goal of culturally relevant mathematics teaching is to move beyond this, as students flourish in doing mathematics when they are connected to the mathematics they learn in authentic ways. But often problem contexts carry implicit cultural assumptions that represent white, middle-class experiences as universal. Authentic experiences in mathematics mean students are able to inquire about themselves and the world around them in familiar and empowering ways. By posing questions that matter to students, they get a sense that mathematics can be used to address and respond to situations in their real life and not just in a textbook.

There is real power in students being able to use mathematics to draw critical conclusions that support their hopes and dreams.

There is real power in students being able to use mathematics to draw critical conclusions that support their hopes and dreams. Harnessing the power of culture and ethnicity in mathematics provides us opportunities to challenge societal issues and norms that limit how historically excluded groups—particularly BIPOC—participate in democracy. We can challenge the inequities that exist in our society *with* mathematics. In general, we will refer to this capacity for action as *agency*. Agency is an essential part of reimagining the mathematics classroom in more authentic ways, which we will talk more about in the next chapter.

AGENCY

Agency in mathematics refers to the ways in which communities of learners are empowered to take individual and collective action in their lives through the mathematics they experience.

In order to help *all* students reach their fullest potential, we must recenter mathematics through the lens of the students themselves and craft experiences that will be relevant and meaningful to them—especially for those who have been historically marginalized.

CULTURALLY RELEVANT TEACHING

Framed by Gloria Ladson-Billings in her seminal book *The Dreamkeepers* (2009), *culturally relevant pedagogy (CRP)* describes how teachers utilize culture and community to empower students intellectually, socially, emotionally, and politically. There are three essential markers of practice for CRP:

Academic success	The success that students experience as a result of classroom instruction and learning experiences
Cultural competence	Centering student culture in teaching and learning as culture and community are affirmed and celebrated
Critical consciousness	Empowering students to challenge inequity, give voice to justice as they learn, practice empathy, and work in solidarity toward collective action

IMAGINE

How does a vision of culturally relevant teaching challenge what you see as effective mathematics teaching?

CRP allows us to reimagine and re-create what is possible for students in mathematics for several reasons. For one, it challenges us to examine our beliefs about race, ethnicity, and culture. This means reflecting on our beliefs about the nature of mathematics, whose math it is, and for whom it works. It also requires us to explore our mathematical histories, trauma, or privilege arising from our experiences while we consider those of our students.

We want teachers to become experts in the design of practical experiences to support powerful culturally relevant teaching in mathematics. In our work over the years, we have observed and documented how teachers struggle when they are left to design these kinds of authentic mathematics experiences for their students without adequate tools and support (Matthews, 2003; Matthews, Jones, & Parker, 2013; Jones, 2015). In the chapters that follow, we wish to help teachers to accomplish three things:

1. Understand key tenets of culturally relevant mathematics teaching

2. Explore strategic approaches for designing culturally relevant mathematics tasks

3. Constantly refine and improve their work on this journey

Consider the following vignette and how it encompasses culturally relevant mathematics teaching.

VIGNETTE 2: ADDRESSING HOMELESSNESS IN THE COMMUNITY TASK

Mrs. Herrington planned an eighth-grade math unit to increase her students' awareness of the growing homeless population in their city. First, students shared experiences they have encountered related to people experiencing homelessness and ways they have seen people help unhoused persons. In groups, they discussed and then shared factors that might influence homelessness. For the activity, students will research data about their city, including the median income, the median annual rent, and the change in the unhoused population over the last 5 to 10 years. They will graph the relationship between the data and determine equations for each graph. They will look at trends in the data. Based on these factors, students will discuss their findings and brainstorm ideas of what community leaders could do to reduce the number of people experiencing homelessness in their city. Students can also discuss what actions, if any, they could take to help their neighbors experiencing homelessness. (See CCSSM standards 8SP2, 8SP3.)

Source: Adapted from www.Citizenmath.org with permission

ASK

Reflect and discuss how the three hallmarks of culturally relevant teaching are reflected in this vignette. What follow-up lessons might be possible from this vignette? In what ways is this kind of teaching similar to or different from what you have experienced? Can you share other examples of culturally relevant teaching?

FUNDAMENTALS OF CULTURALLY RELEVANT TEACHING OF MATHEMATICS

Our vision of culturally relevant mathematics teaching draws from both mathematics reform goals and cultural and social justice approaches to teaching, working together to radically transform student outcomes and quality of life (Enyedy & Mukhopadhyay, 2007; Gutstein et al., 1997; Leonard & Guha, 2002; Matthews, 2003; Tate, 2004). Although culturally relevant teaching in general can include a myriad of teaching styles from traditional to modern, we stress connections with modern mathematics expectations that represent the educators we serve. Gutstein and colleagues (1997) denoted important connections for math reform and culturally relevant teaching, namely (1) fostering critical mathematical thinking as well as critical consciousness; (2) building on students' informal mathematics knowledge and their cultural knowledge; and (3) promoting empowerment orientations to students' culture and experience rather than deficit orientations.

In the following vignette, Mr. Canton uses mathematics to explore resources during the COVID-19 pandemic.

VIGNETTE 3: RESOURCEFULNESS DURING THE PANDEMIC

Image source: iStock.com/Maridav

During the pandemic, it was difficult to find hand sanitizer. Mr. Canton used a recipe to have his sixth-grade students make their own hand sanitizer at home. He found a recipe for 4 ounces of hand sanitizer: Use 7 tablespoons plus 1 teaspoon of 70% isopropyl alcohol and 2 teaspoons of aloe vera gel. You can also add 8 to

10 drops of essential oil (to make it smell good) and 5 drops of vitamin E oil (for a moisturizer). Mr. Canton had the students work in groups to determine how much of each ingredient was needed to make a batch large enough for their class of 25 students. Each student will receive a small 3.4 ounce bottle of hand sanitizer. What total amount did the class make? What is an essential oil? Which one would your group choose and why? What is a better way to keep your hands clean?

When the pandemic hit in 2020, the public had to learn to do more with less. Many items in grocery stores were out of stock, had exorbitant pricing, or were rationed. It is important to teach students how to be resourceful during times like this. By helping students to see that they can, in fact, make their own hand sanitizer, Mr. Canton is helping them to see how they can take care of themselves and help their families get through a difficult situation. This type of assignment empowers students to see themselves as producers and not merely consumers. This experience helps to foster student agency.

As mathematics teachers engage in culturally relevant mathematics teaching, they are committing to the design of mathematics environments as extended, interconnected spaces centered in the realities of students' racial/cultural identities and communities (Matthews, 2009). In this way, teachers will design lessons that center, extend, and connect with students' racial and cultural identities and communities. They also attend to the organization of instruction in ways that underscore deliberate, empowering relationships with students and community. Teachers who engage in this kind of teaching also work to select, design, and use mathematics tasks that highlight students' experiences through cultural and community inquiry. Finally, they often challenge and enhance mathematics curricula in creative ways. In summary, we are defining culturally relevant mathematics teaching as teaching that is focused on these three things:

1. Challenging mathematics experiences where students have access and are positioned as successful doers and creators of mathematics.

2. Mathematics contexts, prompts, and inquiry from culture and community sources.

3. Activity/task outcomes for hope, empathy, and critical agency as students practice mathematics.

RIGOR AS A FLOOR FOR INTELLECTUAL AND CULTURAL MATHEMATICS EXPERIENCES

The foundational principle of culturally relevant teaching is *academic success*. Academic success in mathematics is an equity movement cornerstone. It demands the provision of full access to high-quality math experiences for BIPOC students (and all students) in mathematics. Here, students are viewed as capable of engaging intellectually as doers *and producers* of mathematics and are afforded the environment where this is possible. This should also include access to high-quality design of learning experiences as well as a commitment to mathematics learning immersed in culture.

---

*Students deserve access to mathematical complexity
regardless of race, culture, and/or identity.*

Rigor is an important component of high-quality learning. We refer to rigor in the intellectual sense as having sufficient *mathematical complexity* and, as such, placing *meaningful cognitive demands* on the learner. Access to mathematical complexity is critical to the success of learners in school, which then extends to their day-to-day life activities and ultimately the access they will have to many careers. Students deserve access to mathematical complexity regardless of race, culture, and/or identity. We hold that it should be seen as a baseline requirement for engaging in high-quality mathematics, not a ceiling. As we journey on, we are also careful to expand the notion of rigor to that of culture as well.

We also want you to challenge rigor beyond intellect. Another way of looking at rigor is to think beyond notions of intellectual challenge. We also expand rigor as *careful deliberate attention to student culture and community*—that is, rigor refers to an embracing of complexity, both intellectual and relational.

CULTURE AND COMMUNITY AS A CENTRAL SOURCE OF MATHEMATICS ACTIVITY

Using what students know and have experienced previously is an important feature of effective mathematics teaching, as highlighted in NCTM's *Principles and Standards for School Mathematics* (2000). Understanding the source of student knowledge and placing students' culture and experience at the center of mathematics learning is critical to engaging them in mathematics. We borrow the phrase *building on students' informal and cultural knowledge* (Gutstein et al., 1997) to describe how teachers use cultural knowledge as a part of understanding prior experiences. These informal, cultural math experiences can be found in the home and extend into community culture. We'll talk more about the *how* throughout the book.

Understanding the source of student knowledge and placing students' culture and experience at the center of mathematics learning is critical to engaging them in mathematics.

A mistake teachers and other educators often make is that they consider learning to be an individual process, ignoring the importance of cultural and social influences. Further to the point, constructivism, the dominant learning theory embraced by many mathematics educators and promoted in mathematics education reform, has been criticized for its sole emphasis on individual differences at the expense of social and cultural differences (see Taylor, 1996; Zevenbergen, 1996). The promise of culture-centered approaches to teaching rests in the understanding of how cultural identity, practices, beliefs, and worldviews exist and are shaped in communities. Students (and teachers) are all members of complex, intersectional, and dynamic community groups. An understanding of these "collective" forces, at the same time recognizing individuals, is an important component of drawing from cultural spaces for mathematics activity.

Are you a member of the community where your school is located? If not, it can be helpful to compare your own community to that of your students. The following is a simple activity that can help you start getting more familiar with the community and culture of your students.

One day on your way to work, take notice of how many of the establishments listed in Figure 1.3 you pass in your neighborhood compared to the number near your school.

CREATE

Choose a movie or cultural media artifact that represents a powerful narrative of the informal experiences of your students. Make a list of experiences depicted in the artifact that resonate. Identify at least three ways in which mathematics learning might be built from these experiences.

ASK

Is learning individual or cultural? What are the implications of either view for teaching mathematics?

FIGURE 1.3 ● Community Walk checklist

ESTABLISHMENT	TALLY IN YOUR COMMUNITY ------- Circle One: Rural, Urban, Suburban	TALLY IN SCHOOL COMMUNITY ------- Circle One: Rural, Urban, Suburban
Churches, mosques, temples, and other places of worship		
Liquor stores		
Grocery stores		
Check-cashing businesses		
Playgrounds		
Multi-family buildings (i.e., apartments, duplexes, etc.)		
Doctor/dentist offices		
Urgent care locations/walk-in clinics		
Laundromats		
Hair salons/barber shops		
Community centers		
Shopping malls or shopping centers		
Empty lots		
Dollar stores		
Gas stations		
Fast food restaurants		

MATHEMATICS AS A PRACTICE OF CRITICAL AGENCY AND ACTION

Teaching mathematics in a way that redefines critical thinking for students within and outside of the school setting is another important connection for standards-based mathematics reform with culturally relevant pedagogy. Critical consciousness involves being able to look critically at knowledge, school, and society with regard to the roles each has played in the miseducation, domination, and marginalization of people-groups (Ladson-Billings, 1994, 1995).

Correspondingly, critical mathematical thinking includes "making conjectures, developing arguments, investigating ideas, justifying answers, validating one's thinking" (Gutstein et al., 1997, p. 718). Therefore, a critical consciousness motive—critical agency—in mathematics learning allows teachers to help students expand their critical mathematical thinking in ways that challenge inaccurate knowledge and question unjust societal and schooling practices and policies.

PLAN

Based on the variety of establishments you passed the closer you got to your school, what does that say about the community in which your students live? How can you use that information to create empowering tasks for your students?

VIGNETTE 4: RURAL SCHOOL DISTRICT MATHEMATICS TASK

Mr. Aizawa works in a rural regional school district in a small northeastern state. As part of a lesson on unit rates, he explored with his students the equity of access to health care in rural areas. The students started class by having a discussion with their groups of what a primary care physician (PCP) is. Then, they discussed what it means to live in a rural area. This led to a class discussion of how far each student travels to see their family doctor. Mr. Aizawa was surprised to find out that about half of his students reported only going to walk-in clinics when they are sick. Some other students reported driving at least 30 to 40 minutes to the larger city to see a doctor. Students worked in groups to find the population of selected counties in their state and the corresponding number of PCPs in each of those counties. Mr. Aizawa asked students why just reporting the number of PCPs was not enough to determine an inequity.

IMAGINE

How might this lesson end? What do you think the students learned about their community in this lesson? What mathematics helped them to understand this issue? What further justice actions might this work lead to for students?

Summary and Discussion Questions

In this chapter, we shared expectations of modern mathematics and fundamental ideas to culturally relevant mathematics teaching. In particular, expectations for modern mathematics include shifts in mathematics learning, teacher roles, and the meaningfulness of mathematics. We also discussed ideas that are fundamental to culturally relevant mathematics teaching:

1. Challenging mathematics experiences where students have access and are engaged as successful doers and creators of mathematics.
2. Mathematics contexts, prompts, and inquiries drawn from culture and community.
3. Intentional task outcomes and environments centered on hope, empathy, and critical agency as students practice mathematics.

First, students deserve access to mathematical complexity regardless of race, culture, and/or identity as a *baseline* requirement for engaging in high-quality mathematics—that is, rigor is a *floor*, not a ceiling. Also, culture and community are central sources of mathematics activity, reinforcing the idea that powerful mathematics learning is centered in the individual and collective cultural identities students bring to instruction. And finally, mathematics is a practice of critical agency, which allows mathematics teachers to help students expand their critical mathematical thinking in ways that challenge inaccurate knowledge and question unjust societal and schooling practices and policies. Before we explore and expand the features of culturally relevant mathematics tasks and practices in the next chapter, consider the following discussion questions to reflect on the topics we just covered:

1. How would you respond when asked about the nature of mathematics and how it should be taught? What are some ways that mathematics and culture complement each other?
2. How would you describe the student cultures at your school? List some ways you might tap into the richness, uniqueness, and diversity of those cultures to enhance your mathematics instruction.
3. What is one current social issue in your students' communities, and how could you use mathematics to illuminate that issue for students?
4. What adjustments have you made or can you make as a teacher to take on a less active role, encouraging students to be co-creators in the problem-solving process?
5. How do you create a space where students can take a more active role as collaborators?

CHAPTER 2

Imagining Culturally Relevant Teaching Through Mathematics Practices and Tasks

In this chapter, we will

- Expand the definition of mathematics tasks
- Explore culturally relevant mathematics practices
- Illuminate the importance of mathematics tasks in creating culturally relevant mathematics experiences
- Explore features of culturally relevant, cognitively demanding mathematics tasks

Mathematics tasks are the chief means for how students participate and experience math in the classroom. Yet too many students face unimaginative, cookie-cutter experiences drawn from paid websites, picked up in staff lounges, or copied from stock textbooks. While all of these are legitimate sources for tasks, we often see missed opportunities here for teachers to fully embrace the power of the instructional core.

The instructional core consists of three active components: (1) what the teacher *says* and *does*, (2) what students *say* and *do*, and (3) the task *structure* and *design* as utilized by the teacher. At any given time, these dynamics are activated in the classroom. With each of the core components, the teacher is directly responsible for how students engage mathematics through the task, discourse, and interactions rising out of the classroom. In the following sections, we'll explore why and how tasks are great platforms for culturally relevant teaching and provide a catalyst for cognitive challenge in mathematics.

One of the questions we consistently encounter in our work with teachers is, What does this look like in practice? To answer this question, we will explore examples of what students might do, show how tasks support culturally relevant teaching, and provide a list of features of culturally relevant mathematics tasks.

EXPANDING THE STRUCTURE OF MATHEMATICS TASKS

Before we begin the design process for creating culturally relevant mathematics tasks, let's expand the definition of mathematics tasks. According to Stein et al. (1996), a mathematical task is defined as a single problem or a set of problems that focuses student attention on a mathematical idea. As we focus on the structure of a task, we seek to name what we believe are key parts to many of the mathematics tasks that teachers come into contact with. For purposes of understanding the structure of math tasks, we want to look at four organized dimensions that we feel encapsulate the mathematical and social/cultural constraints of math tasks used in the classroom:

1. Mathematics Constraints and Conditions
2. Mathematical Inquiry Prompt
3. Cultural Context
4. Cultural Inquiry Prompt

MATHEMATICS CONSTRAINTS AND CONDITIONS

Mathematics constraints represent the content, language, and representations that define problem constraints (limitations on a solution approach), mathematical assumptions, and conditions that help the learner home in on key concepts and procedures needed to unlock the mathematics inquiry. In short, the "constraint" frames the boundaries of the content. In saying "The equation gives the height (h) of the ball at any time (t)," the doer is tasked with finding that the value of the height (from a ball thrown) when given the relationship (function) between the height of an object at any given time is $-16t^2 + 40t + 1.5$.

MATHEMATICAL INQUIRY PROMPT

The first element we define is what many will see as most common to any mathematics task: the *mathematical prompt*. A mathematical prompt is a specific question or direction for which the problem doer must directly respond or engage. Take, for example, this seventh-grade task: *Write three ratios that are equivalent to the one given: The ratio of right-handed students to left-handed students is 18:4.* The phrase "write three ratios" represents the mathematical prompt, urging the doer to search for equivalent ratios.

CULTURAL CONTEXT

Mathematics tasks and applications are typically situated in some kind of context to help students make sense of the task and relate it to the real world. We explicitly label this as cultural and argue that all mathematics—as all human knowledge—is inherently cultural and social. *Cultural contexts*, therefore, are settings and situations in which mathematical tasks are embedded and are given for the purpose of assisting learners to draw from hopefully familiar referents when tackling mathematical ideas. Cultural contexts include the explicit, implied, or hidden values and practices of a particular culture. Culture can be relevant to specific ethnicities, cultural groups, and communities. We see culture in this sense as dynamic, fluid, boundless, and intersectional. In Figure 2.1, the cultural context is that of shooting a cannon, possibly for sport. The context itself is fluid and not absolutely an element solely of a particular group. The many ways in which this context can be interpreted should be seen as an asset in creating culturally relevant experiences.

> **CULTURAL CONTEXTS**
> Settings and situations in which mathematical tasks are embedded and are given for the purpose of assisting learners to draw from hopefully familiar referents when tackling mathematical ideas.

SOCIOCULTURAL INQUIRY PROMPT

The *sociocultural prompt* provides specific direction or requirement for the learner to address social, cultural, and political conditions in the context. The presence of a sociocultural prompt is an opportunity to engage in both cultural competence and critical consciousness—two key components of culturally relevant teaching. Sociocultural prompts can be extracted from common character and ethics programs already in schools, as well as from important historical accounts and current social and political events. We see good prompts as those that ask students to inquire culturally and socially.

> **SOCIOCULTURAL PROMPT**
> Provides specific direction or requirement for the learner to address social, cultural, and/or political conditions in the context.

In the velocity problem in Figure 2.1, the cultural context, mathematics constraints/conditions, sociocultural prompt, and mathematical prompt are given:

FIGURE 2.1 ● Sample structure of a mathematics task

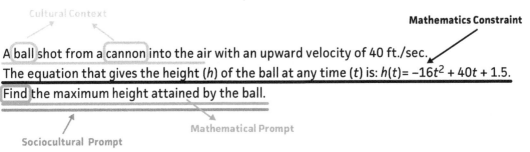

The social prompt isn't obvious in Figure 2.1. It's not absent; it's just that we consider it light—that is, the task simply requires that the doer be concerned about the location of the ball in the context of the ball being shot from a cannon. This is a good example of what we see so often with so many passive math problems in practice. We'll continue to argue in the book that sociocultural prompts are powerful (often missed) opportunities to engage the world around them.

FIGURE 2.2 ● Sample structure of a mathematics task

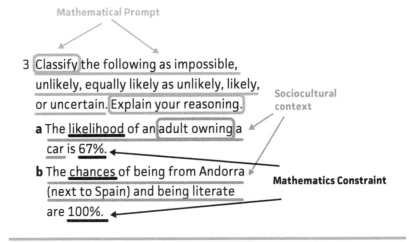

In Figure 2.2, the doer is prompted to analyze the likelihood of a series of events and is given suggested probabilities as a basis of the analysis. From a sociocultural perspective, the context of the two scenarios involve two areas of human experience: (1) car ownership and (2) ethnicity and literacy. While this is a better example than the previous problem in terms of cultural context, the doer is still not prompted to inquire into the nature of the human experience, nor to relate this experience to a personal context or to a state of thriving.

ASK

Choose four tasks from your current curriculum or practice and conduct an analysis of the structure using the four elements. Do they seem to be missing any of the elements? If so, which one(s)? How might you include those missing elements? Which element seems strongest?

WHEN STUDENTS THRIVE: CULTURALLY RELEVANT MATHEMATICS PRACTICES

Our journey to explore what culturally relevant mathematics teaching looks like for students starts with *practices*. In 2020, a team of educators worked on a national project to challenge and extend how popular *mathematics practices* (known widely as Common Core Mathematics Practices) can integrate important elements of authentic human experience similar to the ways in which children experience art, music, or play. This 100Kin10 Project Team created five practices to describe the ways in which children might experience mathematics authentically:

1. Center Complex Identities
2. Expand Understandings
3. Engage Human Experience
4. Fight for Justice
5. Leverage Voice

Taken together, the *Culturally Relevant Mathematics Practices* (Figure 2.3) envision mathematics learning, whether in a face-to-face classroom setting, virtual online space, or some hybrid, as a space where learners thrive and find voice and meaning in the mathematics that they do.

FIGURE 2.3 ● Culturally relevant mathematics practices

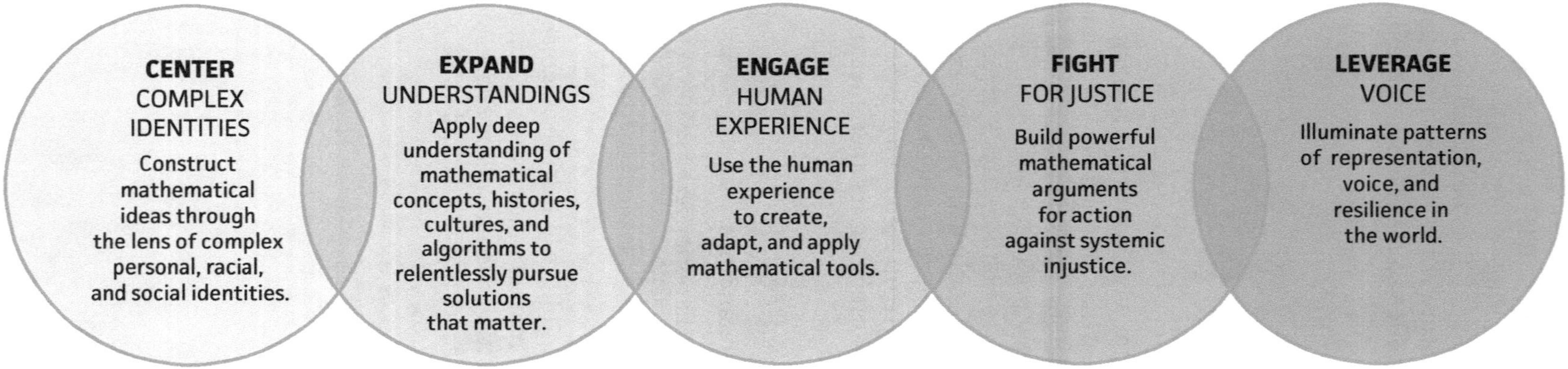

CENTER COMPLEX IDENTITIES
Construct mathematical ideas through the lens of complex personal, racial, and social identities.

EXPAND UNDERSTANDINGS
Apply deep understanding of mathematical concepts, histories, cultures, and algorithms to relentlessly pursue solutions that matter.

ENGAGE HUMAN EXPERIENCE
Use the human experience to create, adapt, and apply mathematical tools.

FIGHT FOR JUSTICE
Build powerful mathematical arguments for action against systemic injustice.

LEVERAGE VOICE
Illuminate patterns of representation, voice, and resilience in the world.

Let's take a look at each of these practices in more depth.

CENTER COMPLEX IDENTITIES

With *Centering Complex Identities*, learners draw from their own identity and those of others as they seek to make sense of mathematical ideas, solve problems, and probe contexts and nuances of the solutions and applications with which they engage.

VIGNETTE 5: #MUSLIM

When working with a group of middle schoolers who participated in a summer STEM program, the teacher led an icebreaker activity that involved students describing themselves through the use of hashtags. Each student was given the opportunity to present one of their hashtags. When one student shared #Muslim, another student unmuted his technology and said, "I'm Muslim too." Later on in a mathematics activity, students shared a photo of something in their home or community that represented mathematics. Maryam, the student who shared the #Muslim hashtag, posted a photo of a sofa in her living room that had an Islamic tessellation design. This scenario provides a wealth of opportunity for the teacher to use this student's ethnic and religious identity to teach a lesson about the geometric transformations that exist in Islamic tessellations as well as other tessellations that students discover in their surroundings and/or create.

Although this vignette happened during a summer STEM program, it can serve as a lesson to classroom teachers. These students were new to each other, but a simple hashtag activity opened up a space for them to connect. Coupled with the follow-up activity of finding geometric transformations, this teacher had the opportunity to center an activity on one or more students' racial and personal identities. These students have a personal connection to mathematics that may have been missed if not for a brief student identity activity. When students are able to bring themselves fully into the mathematics classroom, they don't have to ask, "When am I ever going to use this?"

IMAGINE

Imagine a mathematics scenario where students explore or inquire about various aspects of their identity and belonging. How well do the mathematics and identity explorations work together?

EXPAND UNDERSTANDINGS

Expanding Understandings at the secondary level is especially powerful because it is focused on how learners understand mathematics deeply to include histories, cultures, and ways of knowing, along with the understanding of concepts and algorithms.

When students are learning a mathematics concept, they want to understand it deeply, and they are willing to ask questions as long as they know their questions will be considered. Students can tell the difference between a teacher who doesn't answer questions because they want you to find a way to answer on your own versus a teacher who makes you feel inadequate because you are asking too many questions. We have found that students prefer to do mathematics when they can do it their own way—that is, when they are empowered to discover the solution themselves. When students are provided the opportunity to do it their own way, the mathematics comes from the student; they are not merely mimicking the teacher. When students are required to follow a procedure exactly how the teacher does, the student learns that the teacher alone is responsible for mathematical sense making. They may be less inclined to take intellectual risks or demonstrate curiosity about contexts and application. For example, many secondary classrooms follow the same routine: The teacher lectures/teaches a topic; students take notes or practice problems alone or in small groups; and the teacher calls on students to report on their solutions. Following this routine day-in and day-out forces students to learn that mathematics always comes from an authority like the teacher (and/or the textbook) and not from themselves.

VIGNETTE 6: WHOSE REAL WORLD

Image source: iStock.com /Chalffy

Mr. Eaton wants his sixth-grade students to solve real-world mathematics problems involving area, volume, and surface area. He wants his students to learn through doing rather than through him lecturing and students solving so-called "real-world" word problems. This is a dilemma that many teachers face. Mr. Eaton decides to ask students about interesting things they are doing these days. Many of the students talk about making TikTok videos and learning about the latest Y2K fashions. Mr. Eaton's idea is to have students create TikTok videos using a step and repeat backdrop banner and props with certain constraints. Students can choose a banner size appropriate to their video shoot (8 ft. × 5 ft. or 8 ft. × 8 ft.). They will need two creative logos between 9 and 11 inches in width to showcase their message. They will also need at least two large cubes as props. The cubes will be covered with an original Y2K-inspired fabric. Students will need to show all the work they used to determine the number of logos they need for their backdrop and the amount of fabric needed for their props. If time and space allow, students can create one of the backdrops, film the videos, and present the mathematics associated with proper creation of the video set.

Students enjoy multiple means of engagement, representation, action, and ways of expressing their understanding. When they are able to use their interests to show their understanding of mathematics concepts, they develop confidence and positive mathematical identities. They can relate math to their own lives because they were given the freedom and respect to embody it in themselves.

ENGAGE HUMAN EXPERIENCE

Engaging Human Experience (along with *Fighting for Justice* and *Leveraging Voice*) provides opportunities for learners to explore mathematics problems that are encased in social and community issues, extending the students' roles as problem solvers beyond "neatly" curated pizza or chocolate bar problems.

Responsive learners who embrace *Engaging Human Experience* use mathematics models and tools as important ways to uplift and cherish the human experience. For example, students can explore the many ways in which cultures and communities use mathematics in their daily routines. Students might learn how hair stylists use mathematical ideas in their hair-braiding techniques, how mathematics and art are closely connected, how musicians use mathematics, and the mathematics involved in safe driving, to name a few.

The COVID-19 pandemic, with its waves of deaths, social lockdowns, and economic upheaval, served as a catalyst in reexamining the role of the human experience in learning. Some teachers used this time as an opportunity for students to use human experience to create, adapt, and apply mathematical models. For example, the Common Core Math

Content Standard 7.G.B.6 asks students to solve real-world and mathematical problems involving area, volume, and surface area of two- and three-dimensional objects composed of triangles, quadrilaterals, polygons, cubes, and right prisms. Over the pandemic, many families spent more time together—taking walks, riding bicycles, and overall spending more time outdoors—which was a great opportunity to ask students to notice the mathematics in their community. Students could notice homes as a composite of rectangular and triangular prisms, a water tank as a cylinder, and a perfectly shaped evergreen tree as a cone. They could be encouraged to engage with the world around them while using this information in the mathematics classroom to model "things in our community."

Image source: iStock.com/kali9

ASK

What are three concrete ways your students might uplift and cherish the human experience through mathematics?

FIGHT FOR JUSTICE

Middle and high school students have very important perspectives on justice and fairness in the world. When teachers want to engage students in teaching mathematics with a social justice lens, they should design student-centered math opportunities based on their students' social interactions with the world. When students are bullied, they know it is not fair. When students recognize that their Black classmates are underrepresented in advanced math classes, they sense injustice. Students explore issues such as poverty and racism in their English/language arts and history/social studies classes, but too often these essential topics are left out of math lessons. In mathematics, teachers can broach these difficult topics by first asking students what issues they'd like to learn more about and then using numbers to help students tell a story. We can help students use mathematics to construct viable arguments and critique the reasoning of others (see Math Practice 3) to prove a social and/or racial injustice.

Image source: iStock.com/ProfessionalStudioImages

Sixth-grade teacher Ms. Alvarez shared research by the Centers for Disease Control and Prevention (CDC) that shows more than 32 million U.S. residents have been diagnosed with asthma at some time, while other research shows that in economically stressed U.S. cities, air pollution-related morbidity and mortality are worse than in more prosperous cities. She asked her students to explore this question: Could it be that poor air quality in U.S. cities correlates with more cases of asthma? To answer this question, students will calculate/find the mean, median, and mode for each city and for all of the cities combined using data they find while researching the air quality index (AQI) of selected cities in their state or around the country. Students will discuss the variations in air quality and possible reasons for the variations; then, they will determine which measure of central tendency best describes each city's air quality and why. Students will determine which city has the worst air quality and explain how they made that determination. Students might also collect data on the population of these cities as well as median income.

IMAGINE

What do you think students will notice and wonder while completing this task? What are some ways to provide student voice in bringing attention to this issue? How can students fight for justice in environmental issues that affect them?

LEVERAGE VOICE

If you want to learn about issues that affect students, you must ask them. Students are usually more informed than we give them credit for, and they are full of thoughts, feelings, and opinions about significant issues. To *Leverage Student Voice* in positive ways, we must illuminate patterns of representation, resistance, and resilience in the world. In mathematics, there are many ways to immerse students with positive representations of diverse people. One example of leveraging voice might be when students celebrate the growth of Black medical professionals in their community by calculating percentage increase and decrease. Exploring growth (or decline) in this way opens up the potential to critical conversation in considering access to STEM professions.

Leveraging voice also allows teachers to draw from a variety of resources and media (e.g., www.mathematicallygiftedandblack .com; www.lathisms.org; www.indigenousmathematicians.org) to illuminate collective stories of resistance and resilience in mathematics. One such story can be told about mathematician Gloria Gilmer. She was a pioneer of a branch of mathematics called ethnomathematics. As a mathematician, she could see the mathematics associated with Black women's hairstyles. She saw tessellations and was curious to know more about hair braiding. She visited a hair salon to speak with the stylists and found that the braiding styles followed a pattern of triangular numbers, which consisted of adding consecutive numbers to find the total number of braids when each row of braids had one more braid than the previous row. When teachers bring this information to their classrooms, some students are immediately drawn to it because they can see themselves in the mathematics. The story helps to leverage the voices of some students who traditionally are not highlighted in the mathematics classroom.

Image source: iStock.com/NickyLlyod

TASKS AS OPPORTUNITIES TO BUILD MATHEMATICAL THINKING

We see the critical work in this book as focusing on the mathematics *task*. Inquiring through mathematics tasks provides opportunities for students to practice math in the context of who they are and their relationships to others and the world around them. Modern mathematics reform (as we covered in Chapter 1) requires that teachers identify, create, and even transform traditional mathematics tasks in order to engage students' thinking. These tasks should emphasize the learning of rich mathematics concepts, multiple representations and strategies, and the communication of one's reasoning when problem-solving (NCTM, 2000).

Consider a commonly used example in the Locker Problem.

Image source: iStock.com/Rawf8

A school has exactly 100 lockers, numbered 1 to 100. The principal needs help from her 100 students to close the lockers. She assigns each student a number and asks them to help her, one by one. Student #1 is to open every locker. Student #2 is to close every second locker. Student #3 is to go to every third locker (if closed, open it; if open, close it). Student #4 is to go to every fourth locker (if closed, open it; if open, close it). This goes on until Student #100 is finished. The principal can now go and close any left-open lockers. How many lockers will the principal close?

The Locker Problem is rich because there are multiple strategies and entry points that students can use to solve the problem. Students might draw a picture or graphic to help them. They might make an organized list or act it out. They might use more complex strategies such as creating a table and finding a pattern. Students who are ready could even determine if an equation exists that could generalize the pattern. A teacher could use this type of open-ended problem to create a culture of discourse in the classroom. The multiple entry points allow for all students to engage at different levels, from drawing a picture to creating an equation.

Choosing rich tasks like the Locker Problem provides an opportunity to build students' mathematical thinking. But these tasks can be reengineered to support cultural inquiry, engaging students in investigations formulated in local or cultural context. For example, instead of merely opening and closing lockers, the teacher could include a cultural context about how students feel about not having enough time to get to their locker and to class on time.

NOT JUST ANY TASK: COMPLEXITY MATTERS

In addition to being a platform for culturally relevant teaching, good mathematics tasks provide opportunities to challenge students by exposing them to the "right kind of hard." Challenging students with complexity in the tasks they do raises the bar for modern classrooms. According to the NCTM (2000), tasks that have the most potential to grow student thinking focus on rich mathematical concepts, allow for multiple ways of representing ideas, and require communication. Embracing and building tasks around mathematical complexity leads to important opportunities for learners.

> *Good mathematics tasks provide opportunities to challenge students by exposing them to the "right kind of hard."*

Compare the difference in a task such as the simple written equation of 3 × 5, in which a student is asked to recall a memorized multiplication fact, versus a task that asks students to choose whether three groups of five or five groups of three is the best representation for a given word problem. Both kinds of tasks are necessary, but they offer varying levels of cognitive effort.

ASK

Scan an upcoming mathematics lesson for tasks. Describe the balance of lower cognitive level and higher cognitive level demanding tasks. What do you notice?

In our work with new teachers, we ask them to take note of what Stein et al. (2000) define as *lower-level* and *higher-level* cognitive demand in mathematics tasks. (In general, we use the term "demand" to refer to mathematical complexity.) *Lower-level* tasks typically require less cognitive effort and involve recitation of number facts or using procedures and algorithms in isolation. *Higher-level* cognitively demanding tasks require students to use procedures in ways that build conceptual understanding of important concepts.

In many mathematics textbooks, the percentage of lower-level tasks will typically outnumber the cognitively demanding tasks. The higher-level tasks are often non-algorithmic, unpredictable, and require multiple ways of representing concepts. Open-ended word problems, for example, involve a series of steps and often require representations, including symbolism, graphs, and verbal explanations. Hence, open-ended word problems tend to be on the higher level on the complexity scale.

Another benefit of higher-level tasks is that students often have to draw from their informal experiences to make sense of problem contexts. In the following example, students are able to go from recognizing a pattern in adding consecutive numbers to producing a generalized rule.

Consider Gloria Gilmer's work with the triangular numbers involved in hair braiding *(mentioned earlier in this chapter)*. For 1 row of braids we have 1 braid. For 2 rows, we have 3 braids (1 + 2); 3 rows are 6 braids (1 + 2 + 3), 4 rows are 10 braids (1 + 2 + 3 + 4), and so on. How many braids in 5 rows? 10 rows? N rows?

ROW OF BRAIDS	NUMBER OF BRAIDS IN ROW	TOTAL NUMBER OF BRAIDS
1	1	1
2	1 + 2	3
3	1 + 2 + 3	6
4	1 + 2 + 3 + 4	10
5	1 + 2 + 3 + 4 + 5	?
10	1 + 2 + ... + 9 + 10	?
N	1 + 2 + ... + N	?

Building mathematical thinking supports students in experiencing academic success, a key component of culturally relevant teaching. This not only helps students learn math but also supports another kind of invaluable learning—that of pride and self-esteem.

VIGNETTE 8: REPRESENTATION MATTERS

Growing up, I did not see myself in the math curriculum, and I experienced difficulty establishing a math identity. Recently, I had a meeting with my professor, and during the meeting, the professor took one look at my braids and started telling me about the mathematician Dr. Gloria Gilmer and her study that correlated hair braiding to tessellations. After the meeting, I performed research on Dr. Gilmer and her study. While reading her work, I felt a sense of pride and belonging. Prior to engaging in this research, I never saw myself or my culture represented in math.

The next day, I engineered a lesson for my school where I introduced Dr. Gilmer to my scholars. My scholars and I discussed her study, and I encouraged them to identify other tessellations. While performing this lesson, I immediately noticed that my scholars were engaged and started referring to people who knew how to braid as mathematicians. One scholar, who already wants to be a hairdresser, discussed the intricacies of braiding. She informed us that a hairdresser has to consider variables such as the size of a person's head and the amount of hair necessary to complete each style. Every scholar paid attention to her words and validated her contribution to the lesson.

As the lesson progressed, scholars started to identify tessellations in their community. Oftentimes, scholars from low-income neighborhoods lack self-esteem in regard to where they come from. However, it was a special moment when scholars were able to take pride in their home community as they identified tessellations in the windows of the nearest bodega or hexagons on the pavement downtown.

Learning about Dr. Gloria Gilmer assisted in transforming the lens and dispositions of my scholars. Scholars started seeing their environment as art as opposed to impoverished and thought of themselves as mathematicians as opposed to just people who braid.

—Mrs. Northcutt, Educator and Graduate Student

We do not suggest that teachers avoid low-level tasks altogether. But an important criterion for cultural relevance is the presence of high expectations and the potential for academic success. Challenging students with the "right kind of hard" gives students the best chance of being successful in mathematics.

TASKS AS OPPORTUNITIES TO PRACTICE CULTURALLY RELEVANT TEACHING

Packed within mathematics tasks are messages about what math is and what it means to do mathematics. Also implicit are ideas about context—that is, what is to be valued and for what purposes. Our basis for creating culturally relevant mathematics tasks lies in exposing students to as many higher-level tasks as possible. We see this in many ways as a fundamental element of culturally relevant teaching: that students have access to challenging opportunities through which to thrive and develop. This can happen in several ways. When students are asked to explore relationships between what is happening in real life and the procedure for finding a solution, they have the opportunity to make meaningful social and cultural connections.

In the middle and high school grades, students are often asked to make connections between prior learning in mathematics and new mathematical ideas, as well as between the mathematics they are learning and their real life. There is opportunity here to have students brainstorm things they do at home that could be connected to mathematics—things they like to do, things their families do together, things maybe they don't immediately see a mathematics connection to. This type of activity provides an opportunity for students to share about their home life, which at the secondary level is not always an easy thing to do. It helps students get to know one another and helps the teacher get to know their students. Students' roles at home are part of their identity, so it is important to allow students' whole selves into the classroom. In fact, celebrating their multiple identities helps in their identity development.

In the example that follows, if the student is familiar with mooncakes, a traditional Chinese dessert, they will find a connection between mathematics and real life.

Image source: iStock.com/CQYoung

My mom always makes delicious mooncakes to celebrate the Mid-Autumn Festival. Mooncakes are usually a round-shaped baked pastry with a sweet (like sweet bean paste, lotus seed paste, salted egg yolk) or savory (like ham, Chinese sausage, roasted pork) filling. In order to have a delicious mooncake that doesn't dry out, you must have the correct ratio of sugar to oil. My mom and I expect to make 150 mooncakes to enjoy and to gift to other family members. To make a batch of 12 mooncakes, you will need 100 grams of sugar and 90 grams of canola oil. How much of each ingredient is needed for 150 mooncakes?

Whether or not students personally know about mooncakes, they can use proportions to answer the question about the amount of ingredients and what family members they might gift the desserts. This would also be a great time to query students about their holiday traditions.

Another way tasks provide opportunities for culturally relevant teaching is that they allow for exploring issues and contexts that arise in day-to-day living. By doing this, students can come to appreciate, acknowledge, and learn more about the personal, community, and cultural things that help them thrive and develop. Tasks can also provide the means of helping students respond to challenges of the day, discern patterns, and take stands for social justice and action.

FEATURES OF CULTURALLY RELEVANT MATHEMATICS TASKS

Based on the importance of high-level cognitively demanding mathematics tasks and culturally relevant teaching, let's define *culturally relevant mathematics tasks* as tasks (1) with high cognitive *demand*, (2) where culture and community are the source of math inquiry (*relevance*), and (3) where individual and collective *agency* are the intentional outcomes (see Figure 2.4).

FIGURE 2.4 ● Culturally relevant mathematics task-building actions

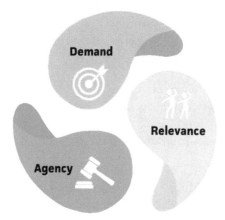

Image source: Demand icon by iStock.com/Fourleaflover; Relevance icon by iStock.com/MicrovOne; Agency icon by /iStock.com/Tanya St

As a more comprehensive list, culturally relevant mathematics tasks

- Are mathematically rich, higher-level cognitively demanding, and embedded in cultural activity.

- Explicitly require students to inquire (at times problematically) about themselves, their communities, and the world around them.

- Include content drawn from students' community and cultural identities and experiences.

- Affirm student belonging and culture—an empowerment and learning orientation (versus deficit or color-blind orientation). Tasks may explicitly seek to add to this knowledge through mathematical activity.

- Ask students to respond to, overcome, and challenge discontinuity and divide between school and their own lives.

- Require students to use mathematics to discuss and make sense of the world around them. The stated goal of the task is to make empowered decisions about themselves, their communities, and the world.

In the next chapter, we will further explore these features and begin to examine how to assess and create culturally relevant mathematics tasks.

Summary and Discussion Questions

In this chapter, we expanded the definition of mathematics tasks; explored Culturally Relevant Mathematics Practices; illuminated the importance of mathematics tasks in creating culturally relevant mathematics experiences; and studied features of culturally relevant, cognitively demanding mathematics tasks.

We presented the following four organized dimensions that encapsulate the mathematical and social/cultural constraints of math tasks used in the classroom: (1) mathematics constraints/conditions, (2) mathematical inquiry prompt, (3) cultural context, and (4) sociocultural inquiry prompt.

Based on the importance of high-level cognitively demanding mathematics tasks and culturally relevant teaching, we define *culturally relevant mathematics tasks* as tasks (1) with high cognitive demand, (2) where culture and community are the source of math inquiry (relevance), and (3) where individual and collective agency are the intentional outcomes. Throughout the book, we will use the idea of Culturally Relevant Mathematics Practices where learners thrive and find voice and meaning in the mathematics that they do.

Before we move on to further explore these features and begin to examine how to assess and create culturally relevant mathematics tasks in the next chapter, consider the following discussion questions to reflect on the topics we just covered:

1. Think of the last powerful lesson you taught and reflect on the following instructional core elements: (1) what the teacher says and *does*, (2) what students *say* and *do*, and (3) the task *structure* and *design*. What opportunities did you have for culturally relevant mathematics teaching? How did you respond to these opportunities?
2. Culturally Relevant Mathematics Practices envision mathematics learning as a space where learners thrive and find voice and meaning in the mathematics that they do. Which of the practices do you find most aligned with what you currently do in your instructional core? Where do you see room for growth?

3. Embracing and building tasks around mathematical complexity leads to important opportunities for learners. Select a task from the lesson you chose in Question 1 and analyze it using the four dimensions presented in this chapter (mathematical constraints/conditions, mathematical inquiry prompt, cultural context, and sociocultural inquiry prompt). What are some important opportunities that your learners experienced in the task?

Creating and Assessing Culturally Relevant Mathematics Tasks

In this chapter, we will

- Identify three actions for culturally relevant mathematics task-building
- Explore mathematics tasks using a rubric for creating culturally relevant mathematics tasks

TASK-BUILDING ACTIONS

In Chapter 2, we ended with a list of features describing culturally relevant mathematics tasks (we'll use the abbreviation CRMTasks going forward). In this chapter, we will dive deeper into the teaching actions that are key to building such tasks. The work behind these features can be summarized into three actions for building CRMTasks (see Figure 3.1):

- Establishing sufficient cognitive *demand* to harness student thinking and engagement
- Centering mathematics activity in/as cultural and community inquiry (*relevance*)
- Targeting empathy, *agency*, and social action as task prompts and outcomes

FIGURE 3.1 ● Culturally relevant mathematics task-building actions

Establish Demand and Access

How does the task focus on building deep conceptual knowledge and prompt children to do and create mathematical knowledge?

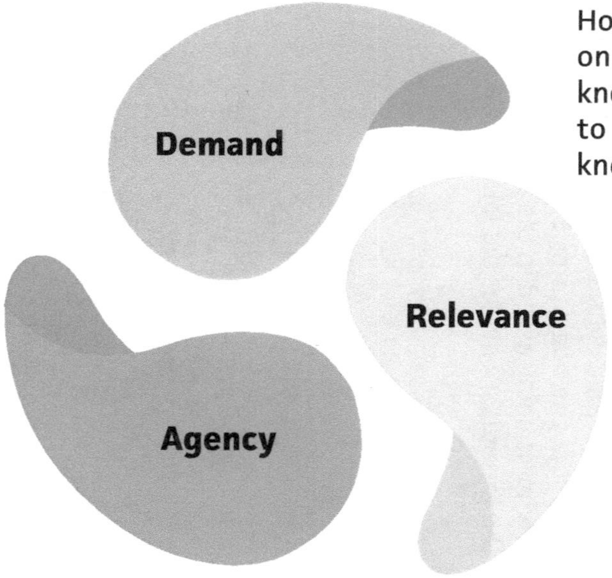

Center Community and Cultural Inquiry

How is the context and mathematical inquiry rooted in affirming and exploring cultural knowledges and identities? Does the task context and prompt feature empowered relationships, understandings about their community, and themselves?

Demand

Relevance

Agency

Target Empathy, Agency, and Social Action

How does the task prompt and context push students to respond to needs and issues with empathy, critical consciousness, and social action?

To access a full-color version of this figure, visit the *Engaging With Culturally Relevant Math Tasks (Secondary)* Free Resources tab on the Corwin website or visit https://bit.ly/3Lgv22E.

online resources

ESTABLISH DEMAND AND ACCESS

We see establishing demand as ensuring that all students are engaging in work that both highlights and strengthens their intellectual power in mathematics. Ladson-Billings (1994) refers to teaching as "mining," where teachers who practice culturally relevant pedagogy (CRP) see—and treat—children as gifted knowledge makers. In mathematics, this requires building prompts and contexts around students' informal, cultural experiences, as well as their prior knowledge. A focus on cognitive demand allows task-builders to consider the cognitive effort required to access knowledge but also grapple with rich mathematical ideas and necessary skills.

Solving problems involving volume of cylinders is a good example of an eighth-grade mathematics topic that can be used to demonstrate cognitive demand in a task. In teaching this topic, it is customary for teachers to provide students with the formula for volume of a cylinder, $V = \pi r^2 h$; however, knowing the formula is just the beginning. Students must then be able to unpack what is being asked in the problem in order to correctly apply the formula. Consider the following activity:

Image source: iStock.com/fcafotodigital

Have students identify one or two of their favorite foods that come in a can. Ask them to answer the following questions:

a. What is the optimal container for one of your favorite foods that comes in a can? Do you think the larger cans are a better buy? Why or why not?

b. Determine the optimal shape of a can to maximize its volume and minimize the materials used to make it.

This optimal-container task requires more thinking than simply calculating volume using a formula because students must show their understanding of how the formula connects to the scenario of volume and price. This requires using prior knowledge of unit rate from grades 6 and 7 to compare cans (cylinders) to determine the best buy. Students will need to measure the height of the cans if that measurement is not already provided. They will also need to measure the diameter of the base of the can, making sure to measure across the center of the circular base, and then divide that in half to get the radius. Once students calculate the volume of each can, they can use that information to determine a unit price for each can. Calculating the unit price for each can will allow students to make comparisons to determine which can and food item is the best buy.

The cognitive demand in this problem requires that students understand what the question is asking. They are not merely following a procedure. In practice, many students have the experience of calculating volume by substituting values into a formula and blindly performing calculations to get an answer, but this does not involve much thinking or understanding of how or why one might reason about the volume of a cylinder. Part B is an extension problem that will require students to consider both volume and surface area, possibly using prior knowledge of nets from sixth grade.

We explained earlier that rigorous mathematical experiences are the floor for high-quality learning. Tasks with higher demands provide opportunities for students to make connections to prior knowledge and draw from relevant contexts. See the following seventh-grade example:

> According to the 2020 census, the population of Arizona was 7,151,502—up from 6,392,017 in the 2010 census. What was the percentage change in the population?

This task requires some degree of cognitive effort from students, and the solution process can be represented in multiple ways (e.g., using a proportion, bar diagram, or the percentage change formula). Students make connections between what they know from sixth grade about ratios and proportional relationships. Additionally, because the concept is introduced in a context, this helps students make connections to why the population is a percentage increase and not a percentage decrease. When students are merely given a formula, $\dfrac{new\ amount - original\ amount}{original\ amount}$, we've found that they might unknowingly switch the order of the values in the numerator, which in turn results in an incorrect sign on the solution. When students merely follow a procedure, they are less likely to make sense of the solution. To strengthen the demand, we could revise the problem to be multistep and also make a stronger sociocultural connection to the students in our classrooms by having them look up the population of their state and have them answer a question of interest to them. For example, students might be interested in how the population growth affected how the school district maps in their city were recently redrawn.

CENTER CULTURAL AND COMMUNITY INQUIRY

One of the most commonly missed opportunities for teachers in creating mathematics activities is in the way contexts are assumed as universal and culturally neutral. Consider the following problem:

Image source: iStock.com/DNY59

Three employees are scheduled to receive holiday bonuses. They have been working for the company for 6, 9, and 15 years respectively. The company announces that it will split $60,000 from a sunshine fund to be shared in the ratio of their years of work experience. Work out the share that each employee receives.

In solving this problem, students calculate individual ratio amounts by finding the total parts (i.e., 6 + 9 + 15 = 30 *total parts*), and then dividing the amount 60,000 by 30 to find the unit share of $2,000, and ultimately provide answers of $12,000; $18,000; and $30,000. Beyond examining the demand of this problem, the problem itself addresses incomes and bonuses that may represent potential opportunities for social inquiry and interrogation. For example, the prospect of receiving a holiday bonus while thinking also about the fairness of the approach of dividing the amount may provide a catalyst in exploring the prevalence and relevance of this practice in real life. There may be wonderings as to whether different allocations might be considered.

> *One of the most commonly missed opportunities for teachers in creating mathematics activities is in the way contexts are assumed as universal and culturally neutral.*

Another example might be the use of the kite, which is commonly featured in high school geometry problems, such as, "Prove the diagonals of a kite are perpendicular." No doubt the kite represents a basic mathematical shape, as pictured in Figure 3.2a. But it is possible to go even further in exploring the social and cultural context of the kite. The notion of flying kites, as is common in many cultural traditions, is a great example of an opportunity to *expand geometry experiences*. The kite problem asks students to think about applying congruence postulates without having to think about kite flying or about the beauty associated with the making of and patterns of kite designs. For example, in Bermuda, Lou grew up flying kites of all shapes with his family members (see Figure 3.2b). In fact, during a visit home to Bermuda he and his niece built a kite using wood, string, and fabric. Consider our two versions of a "kite."

FIGURE 3.2A ● Traditional diamond kite

Image source: iStock.com/Krugli

FIGURE 3.2B ● Traditional Bermuda kite

Image Source: Rebeka Matthews Sousa

IMAGINE

Given the example of the Bermuda kite in Figure 3.2b, can you produce some mathematical ideas that can be explored along with the kite shapes? How might you prepare to use another similar cultural tradition with the students you teach?

When we make the decision to focus on kites in a cultural context, we see additional opportunities for experiencing quality mathematics (in Chapter 6, we pose our "Bermuda kite" problem, for example). In this way, we think of shapes, patterns for design, and even the act of kiteflying itself to explore important math ideas. Indeed, all word problems and contexts carry hidden, assumed cultural ideas and values that are often placed upon students and their teachers. The default for these experiences is to require thinking of mathematics that totally ignores lived experiences. This leads to missed opportunities to challenge and engage students.

The following prompts illustrate more opportunities for cultural and community inquiry.

Prompt 1

Image source: iStock.com/MBPROJEKT_Maciej_Bledowski

What are the pros and cons of a large company like Amazon moving a fulfillment center to your city? Using information about the median annual income in that city, the average annual rent, the unemployment rate, and any other social or economic variables, make a possessive argument for why you might support or not support the move.

Prompt 2

Have you seen people walking around with gallon jugs of water for healthy hydration? According to the U.S. National Academies of Sciences, Engineering, and Medicine, adults should drink between 11.5 and 15.5 cups of water daily. Given this information, what is the best size of a disposable water bottle and why?

Image source: iStock.com/Benjamin Clapp

Prompt 1 models community inquiry and how students might want to learn about the impact of a large company like Amazon moving into their neighborhood. At first glance, it is an exciting prospect for "more jobs," but there are consequences that could be detrimental to the community as well. By learning about these consequences, students can be empowered to speak out for or against this move.

Including a cultural context provides opportunity for students to share similar experiences from their lived experiences and for the teacher to promote inquiry about students' cultures.

IMAGINE

Consider similar word problems for your grade level that you have recently used or seen. Identify the social or cultural context and any prompts that are used to promote inquiry about culture (if any). Think deeply about the opportunities for inquiry. What do you notice? How might you adapt?

An interesting nuance of Prompt 2, the embrace of healthy living, is a powerful message to counter unhealthy eating and obesity in teenagers. It also has the potential to inspire lively discussion about the environmental impact of disposable versus reusable water bottles. Each of these problems offers opportunities for students (and teachers) to inquire and learn.

To target cultural inquiry, ask questions such as these:

- What is the importance of the cultural knowledge/ history implied here?
- What are we curious about?
- What is there to know?
- What can be affirmed?

TARGET AGENCY AND ACTION

By far, the most elusive feature of tasks we see in classrooms has to do with critical agency and consciousness. When we say critical agency, we mean ways in which mathematics experiences require students to respond with empathy, stand in solidarity, explore social issues of justice, and take collective action in community.

AGENCY

Mathematics experiences that require students and teachers to explore social issues of justice, respond with empathy, stand in solidarity, and take collective action in community.

One example of a problem is an eighth-grade task we created comparing soccer salaries. We want to connect with students, but we also want to push students to think more deeply about social issues and issues in their own backyards. For example, we might ask students to explore the past issue of the inequality between women and men in professional soccer through their salaries.

Create two box-and-whisker plots to compare the salaries of the highest-paid women and men soccer players in 2020.

WOMEN (IN U.S. DOLLARS)	MEN (IN U.S. DOLLARS)
518,000	125,000,000
500,000	110,000,000
450,000	95,000,000
447,000	43,000,000
430,000	41,000,000
425,000	35,000,000
400,000	35,000,000
394,500	34,000,000
392,000	32,000,000
380,000	29,000,000

Table: Top Salaries in Soccer in 2020 (https://www.scottfujita.com/soccer/)

a. Draw box-and-whisker plots for each set of data and clearly label the minimum, first quartile, median, third quartile, and maximum.

b. Discuss the spread of the data for each plot. What do you notice about the differences in women's and men's salaries? Are there any outliers?

c. Based on information you gather, develop an argument for the disparity in salaries. How is the issue being addressed? Explore different viewpoints. Protest or defend the vast differences in salaries.

d. In 2022, there was a new labor deal equalizing women's and men's soccer pay in the United States. Create new box plots of top salaries in soccer showing the impact of this historic labor deal. What do you notice?

By having students explore a real social issue, they are pushed to go beyond merely using a data set to create a data display and answer math questions. Issues such as Title IX funding, commercial endorsements, payment to student athletes, and other topics might arise and are opportunities for students to have meaningful conversations about issues they may be experiencing or are familiar with.

To target community action—issues in their own backyards—we might consider the following problem involving a box plot:

A food desert is a neighborhood where there is little or limited access to healthy and affordable food such as fruits, vegetables, whole grains, fresh dairy, and lean meats.

a. Determine the closest food desert to your school or to your neighborhood based on the types of grocery stores and other means of obtaining food.

b. Determine the distance, in miles, to the nearest grocery store from where you live.

c. Have everyone in class write their distances (from home to grocery store) on the board and use the data to create a class box plot.

d. What does the box plot tell you about the neighborhoods in and around our school?

e. Determine possible causes and consequences of food deserts? Work with a partner to produce a solution to the food desert you identified.

We want to connect with students, but we also want to push students to think more deeply about social issues and issues in their own backyards.

In the past, before becoming intentional about the contexts of mathematics tasks we chose, we may have chosen a rigorous math task based on student interest. Creating a box-and-whisker plot of soccer players' heights would be one such problem. But as we learn to move beyond student interest, we are more careful about choosing tasks that provide opportunity for students to think beyond their own interests. Introducing the issue of equal pay for women's and men's sports provides that opportunity.

Students can build agency by exploring such social issues and learning how to use mathematics to make an argument for or against the issue. Targeting agency and action moves us from making an argument to taking action. In particular, we want to provide students with opportunities to take collective action *in* community. By bringing attention to the problem of food deserts popping up in many of our major cities, we are asking students to empathize with the needs of families that live within the food desert perimeter and to explore how this situation was created and how it could be remedied.

IMAGINE

What are some additional experiences or constraints within the food desert problem that could be explored?

RUBRIC FOR CREATING AND ASSESSING CULTURALLY RELEVANT MATHEMATICS TASKS

To help guide teachers as they are beginning to create CRMTasks, we created the *CRCD* (culturally relevant cognitively demanding) *mathematics task rubric* (see Figure 3.3), first published in our chapter in the 2013 book *The Brilliance of Black Children in Mathematics,* Advancing a Framework of Culturally Relevant, Cognitively Demanding Mathematics Tasks. The rubric describes three dimensions through which tasks can be assessed. You will notice that each of the rubric dimensions correlates to one of the task-building actions we have been illustrating in this chapter. With the rubric, we want you to be able to analyze tasks you create, use, or adapt. We acknowledge here that we are talking about assessment long before we have gone into the nuts and bolts of planning. The emphasis is deliberate, as good planning starts with a clear vision of successful outcomes.

The rubric is designed to help educators assess the richness of the mathematics and, equally, the depth of cultural and community knowledge students access in any given task. The rubric has three big considerations for you as a designer. First, it sets a condition that cognitive demand ought to be a baseline for tasks that challenge all students (Emerging/Demand). It can also be seen as a filtering point for revising nonchallenging problems. Second, the rubric also suggests that the educator prioritizes the statement "Good mathematics problems are embedded in cultural and community inquiry and activity!" Thus, designers purposefully center community and culture (Developing/Relevance).

FIGURE 3.3 ● CRCD mathematics task rubric

Requires considerable cognitive effort in mathematics

◇ Task is mathematically rich and cognitively demanding. It requires considerable effort using multiple representations and strategies to develop deep understanding of mathematics. Solution strategy is nonobvious.

◇ Task content draws from connections to other relevant subjects, disciplines, and concepts.

| Emerging |

Requires considerable cognitive effort

AND Embedded in Cultural Self, Community Inquiry, and Activity

◇ Task is centered in real-world situations requiring students to inquire deeply about themselves, their communities, and the world about them.

◇ Requires students to draw from, use, and embrace community and cultural knowledge directly in developing strategy and solution processes.

◇ Task content seeks to add to this knowledge through mathematical activity.

| Developing |

Requires considerable cognitive effort

Embedded in cultural inquiry and activity

AND Targets Cultural Self, Community Empowerment, and Social Justice

◇ Task requires students to examine structure and assumption of self, community, the world, and its relations in consideration of solutions and strategy limits.

◇ Task requires students to examine conditions of opportunity, justice, suffering, and inequity that arise in their communities, school, and the world around them.

◇ Task utilizes mathematical sense making and the solution processes to help students to develop informed perspectives and take action on real-world issues.

| Exemplary |

Third, the rubric challenges us to consider the critical purposes for which mathematics might be defined and used. In other words, the rubric asks educators to assess the possible impact that completion of the task is expected to have on students' lives (Exemplary/Agency).

A few notes for using the rubric. We have repeatedly been asked the question, "Where should I begin?" The answer is simple: The design of CRMTasks can start in any dimension of the rubric. We have also seen in practice that the element of creating a task that provides opportunity to develop students' critical consciousness remains challenging for educators—that is, educators often remain reluctant to address social topics they deem too sensitive or disruptive of the status quo of school mathematics (which is Eurocentric and purportedly culturally/politically neutral). This is a position we reject for several reasons. For one, it doesn't represent the true history of mathematics contributions from various people groups. This position also ignores the very real, lived experiences of many students and their ethnic groups and families; it paints a picture that the world of math does not include them. Acknowledging the experiences of students, as well as their communities of culture and identity, provides agency and voice for all children in mathematics.

IMAGINE

Think of a few tasks you have created or assigned in the past and, based on feedback and reflective experience, analyze them using the rubric. What do you notice?

Our hope is that the rubric offers a progression that helps teachers incorporate social justice issues and critical consciousness into mathematics tasks. We discuss helpful strategies for addressing this challenge in Chapter 6.

EMERGING DIMENSION

We use *Emerging* to define tasks in which all students find challenge, progress, and success. These tasks reflect high-quality features of problem-solving and higher cognitive demand.

Consider the following task as Emerging. It is customary for mathematics textbooks to include problems where students have to find the area of a room's walls to purchase paint. We know that students don't purchase wall paint; however, the context is at least reasonable that students can visualize a room that needs painting.

Mr. Washington wants to purchase paint to paint the walls and ceiling in his living room. The room measures 12 ft. by 18 ft., and the ceilings are 9 ft. high. How much paint does he need, and how much will it cost at $15.48 per gallon with 6% tax? Paint covers 400 square feet per gallon.

Image source: iStock.com/Supersizer

This problem has a high cognitive demand because it will require some degree of cognitive effort. Students must decide what to do with the information provided. Students would already know the difference between area and perimeter, and they would also know that area can be found by multiplying side lengths or by adding using tiling. After they've established that this is a question of area, they can use the area formula to find the total area of the living room. For students who need a visual, they could model the dimensions to help them find the area. Knowledge of what a living room looks like can also help the students to connect the procedure to a context. Once the area is found, students will still need to use decimal multiplication to calculate the cost of the paint.

REFLECT

Looking ahead a bit, what are some features of the *Developing* or *Exemplary* dimensions that are lacking in this problem? For example, how could aspects of cultural inquiry be incorporated?

DEVELOPING DIMENSION

We use *Developing* to define tasks, products, and activities that require students to also engage in cultural and community self-exploration and affirmation. While these tasks represent some progress in design, they are still developing as culturally relevant because they do not prompt students to ask critical questions, beyond surface-level, nor develop critical insights around equity, racial justice, or social justice.

Using local landmarks in the mathematics curriculum is a great way to have students learn about the significance of the landmark and to also make connections between the math they are learning in school and their community. Ms. Lowe works in a school in close proximity to a park where there is an old-fashioned castle that students love to climb. She decided that she would have students calculate the height of tall structures in their school community using angles of elevation, trigonometric ratios, and the Pythagorean theorem. Students will build clinometers using a protractor, straw, string, and paper clip. They will use the clinometers to find the angle of elevation of the structure. Students will work in groups.

Each group will calculate the height of their structure using the tangent function, angle of elevation, and height (from floor to the students' eyes). They will calculate the height of the school building, the flagpole, and the basketball hoop. Each group will answer the following questions:

1. How tall are you? _____ Height from the floor to your eyes: _____

2. Group 1: Stand 10 feet away from the flagpole. What is the angle of elevation? _____

3. Group 2: Stand 5 feet away from the basketball hoop. What is the angle of elevation? _____

4. Group 3: Stand 15 feet away from the school building. What is the angle of elevation? _____

5. Using the tangent function, find the height of your structure. Why does the tangent function work? Draw a picture to show why. Show your math work.

Castle Craig is an observation tower located in Hubbard Park. Betty wants to use her clinometer to figure out how tall Castle Craig is. Betty is standing 12 feet from the base of the tower. She holds her clinometer 5 feet off the ground and measures an angle of elevation of 66 degrees. Draw a picture to show this situation and solve for the height of Castle Craig.

To align this task with the purposes of social justice and empowerment, students should research the significance of the castle structure or other important landmarks in their community.

EXEMPLARY DIMENSION

We use *Exemplary* to define tasks, products, and activities that feature student action, critical investigation, community affirmation, and empowerment notions central to CRMT. Exemplary CRMTasks always have an aspect of students exploring their critical consciousness through contexts that they themselves come up with, such as the overcrowding of their school (Turner & Strawhun, 2007), issues stemming from local inequities like the Flint water crisis (see Aguirre et al., 2019), and racial profiling (Berry et al., 2020; Gutstein & Peterson, 2013), to name a few. All of these topics and many more that have a social justice component should be considered when designing CRMTasks.

In her article "The New Reparations Math," Maya Moore (2020) asked the following question: "Japanese Americans who were victims of WWII internment received an apology and $20,000 reparations from then–President Ronald Reagan. Holocaust survivors received reparations from the German government. What can be gleaned from these historical examples when talking about reparations for slavery in the United States?" Have students research current reparations considerations in California, Oklahoma, or some other discussions such as those by scholar Thomas Craemer, who calculated that reparation payments for American slavery would equal $14 trillion in 2009 dollars. Students should be ready to discuss these questions:

a. What aspects of reparations do you think are involved in making these estimates?

b. What types of formulas might be used, and what factors/variables would be involved?

For the Exemplary dimension Reparations task, we are asking students to critically examine a matter of social justice that has been argued for over 200 years. Where does the United States stand on this issue, and how does any of this discussion affect the future of African Americans? Exemplary tasks, by definition, feature critical investigation of social issues. Reparations for the lasting effects that American slavery has had and continues to have on African American people is certainly a sensitive topic, but it is one that can help to develop *all* students' critical consciousness.

By now, the rubric has been used by hundreds of teachers both to revise existing mathematics tasks to be more culturally relevant and to create new culturally relevant mathematics tasks by considering students' individual and community experiences. Our hope is that teachers continue to use the rubric to guide the overall depth of their task creation work.

When creating CRMTasks, we recognize that there are many ways to start the process. You can begin by considering that students are much like us educators. When we think about important aspects of our lives, we should expect that students have some of the same needs and desires. For example, if you ask someone to choose favorite photos from their cell phone photo gallery, you will most likely see photos of family, friends, pets, and other loved ones. These photos would probably involve the student or adult taking part in activities that are dear to them and that give them joy and pleasure. These activities might take place in their home, sometimes at school, on vacation, visiting family and friends, or as participants at events such as sports, entertainment, and so on. With this in mind, when trying to create CRMTasks, think about and learn about your students' home and community life, cultural traditions, hopes, and hobbies. Do a survey, a Community Walk, or provide opportunities for community members to share their knowledge in your classroom. Current events, important landmarks, and community celebrations can also be used as contexts. We'll discuss some of these opportunities for task creation and others in the next few chapters.

Summary and Discussion Questions

In this chapter, we presented three task-building actions for culturally relevant mathematics tasks: establishing demand; centering community and cultural inquiry; and targeting empathy, agency, and action. We also explored the CRCD (culturally relevant cognitively demanding) mathematics task rubric (see Figure 3.3), which includes three dimensions for creating and assessing culturally relevant mathematics tasks. Having these goals in mind is a useful starting point for creating CRMTasks, and the rubric should help you in determining if you have an Emerging, Developing, or Exemplary task. We used Emerging to define tasks that challenge all students, based on the understanding and assertion that all students are capable of experiencing success. For the next dimension we used Developing to define tasks, products, and activities that require students to also engage in cultural and community self-exploration and affirmation. Finally, we used Exemplary to define tasks, products, and activities that feature student action, critical investigation, community affirmation, and empowerment notions central to CRMT. Before we focus on the planning process for instructional design in the next chapter, consider the following discussion questions to reflect on the topics we just covered.

1. In this chapter, we referred to critical agency as how the task prompt and context require students to respond with empathy, stand in solidarity, explore social issues of justice, and take action. Find a mathematically rich task that you recently used in a lesson or plan to use in an upcoming lesson. What are ways this task can elicit critical agency?

2. List any nonstereotypical cultural connections you can mine from the problem context of the task selected.

3. The rubric presented in this chapter is designed to help educators assess the richness of the mathematics as well as the depth of cultural and community knowledge students access in any given task. Using the same task from Question 1, on what dimension of the CRCD rubric did it initially start? What adaptations can you make to develop the task to the next dimension?

PART II

Practical Approaches for Planning and Creating Culturally Relevant Mathematics Tasks

In the next three chapters, we will describe and explore 12 practical approaches for planning and creating culturally relevant mathematics tasks with hope and intention based on the foundational work of Chapters 1 through 3.

Planning With Intention and Hope

In this chapter, we will

1. Identify three practical approaches in planning the design of a CRMTask

2. Analyze content standards and identify opportunities for culturally relevant mathematics experiences

3. Use the "Hope Wheel" to generate math tasks using "hope" verbs

I relate everything that we basically do. Before I start a topic, I always relate it to a real-life situation. Even if I do problem-solving questions and stuff like that, I relate it to a situation that is happening here. So they can actually see the connection. We do newspaper work, where we take the newspaper and we look for statistics and stuff like that ... and decipher information, so they're learning mathematics, but they are learning in the context.

—Tiffany, middle school teacher

Tiffany was at a crossroads in planning when we talked and had been trying out new flexible ways of approaching lesson planning. She attended a "make mathematics meaningful" workshop one summer and was committed to breaking out of a cycle that included blindly covering objectives. Tiffany's story is not unlike others who feel the burden of needing to make sense of curricular objectives and expectations while simultaneously being concerned with engaging their students. In the next several chapters, we want you to unpack specific actions as you begin creating, adapting, and improving CRMTasks. This process starts at the planning stage, and as all teachers know, planning starts with intentional goals. We want teachers to think about the goals behind tasks as a fundamental first step in creating a task. Goal setting for a given task or task set is one of the most important ways that teachers can plan and account for mathematical experiences that will inspire and empower their students. In this chapter, we offer three practical approaches to help you in planning the intention and content of CRMTasks:

- Unpacking standards for CRMTask-building opportunities
- Adapting content standards with hope verbs
- Creating task goals from hope verbs

Goal setting for a given task or task set is one of the most important ways that teachers can plan and account for mathematical experiences that will inspire and empower their students.

We will work through several examples to help you visualize what it looks like when you intentionally plan for tasks that foster demand, relevance, and agency. We'll also explore how curriculum standards can be leveraged to foster high cognitive demand, cultural relevance, agency, and social justice through mathematics tasks. Finally, we'll share the Hope Wheel (Figure 4.6), a verb-generation model for focusing tasks with intention.

UNPACKING STANDARDS FOR CRMTASK-BUILDING OPPORTUNITIES

Unpacking and transforming curriculum standards represent real opportunities to plan for culturally relevant teaching. We see ways in which analyzing standards can help teachers emphasize and manifest critical moments for agency and inquiry. Another way to approach curriculum standards is to understand that not all standards are equal; some are more ideal for maximizing opportunities for culturally relevant teaching than others. We want to highlight examples of these standards and examine features that directly and indirectly align to CRMTasks so that you are equipped to differentiate standards this way yourself. We also recognize that no educational environment is the same; teachers, curriculum planners, and coaches have varying levels of freedom within which they can create and use tasks in the context of larger standards.

Unpacking and transforming curriculum standards represent real opportunities to plan for culturally relevant teaching.

Most implemented mathematics activities in classrooms are driven by local, regional, and national "standards." The *Common Core State Standards* and the *Massachusetts Curriculum Framework Standards for Mathematical Content* are examples of this. Rigid adherence to standards is often cited by educators as a major obstacle for creating and using CRMTasks. It might be helpful to reframe this obstacle as a question: Are there standards that naturally have greater utility for creating tasks of demand, relevance, and agency? We think so! Let's start by exploring sample standards and provide a brief analysis of how these standards fit.

Consider the following Common Core State Standard:

FIGURE 4.1 ● Potential task-building actions of middle and high school math standards

Having the doer weigh possible outcomes and assigning probabilities can lead to experiences requiring deep reflection, flexible thinking, and multiple representations, emphasizing cognitive demand.

CCSS.MATH.CONTENT.HSS.MD.B.5
(+) Weigh the possible outcomes of a decision by assigning probabilities to payoff values and finding expected values.

The opportunities to consider the outcomes of decision-making point to the possibilities of considering human experiences and the impact of decisions made in the "real world."

In Figure 4.1, we see how this standard looks when we correlate it with our model for task-building actions (in Figure 4.1, blue = Demand, gray = Relevance, light blue = Agency). This is how we can evaluate the potential of the standards as a basis for a culturally relevant mathematics task.

In our quick parse of this standard, several points stand out. First, you will notice how the standard outlines student thinking about the mathematical concept of probability, making room for big ideas, multiple representations, reasoning, and applications. This scope of math content and activity will be important in establishing demand for tasks. We see this in many iterations of standards and curriculum objectives—the challenge for teachers is then to choose instructional mandates that underscore cognitive demand.

Second, the standard also opens the door for students to delve into "real-world" problems (Relevance). "Real world" can be thought of as code for ensuring tasks are authentic and engaging. However, if our goal is to create truly culturally relevant math tasks, it's essential that we ask whose "real world" we are considering. In thinking about the real world, there is opportunity in planning to consider relevant issues and contexts that each student might directly identify with and be inspired by. Reframing it in this way allows for opportunities to create or adapt contexts that are local, known, and cherished by students.

The term "real world" also carries opportunities to focus on critical issues that potentially help students to exercise critical consciousness and responsiveness as citizens (Agency). We should note that many teachers feel hesitancy and sometimes outright resistance in exploring student agency as "real world." If that describes you, this can be an opportunity to investigate your reluctance and explore the choices you can make to better align your teaching methods with your intentions as a culturally minded and inclusive educator.

A common misconception is that real-world contexts are automatically and inherently culturally relevant. Real-world contexts are culturally relevant when they feature authentic cultural and community inquiry *and* if they target social agency and action. This aspect of task-building requires an intentional effort.

CREATE

Find a curriculum standard from your grade level or math content area like the one shown in Figure 4.1. Create a "real-world" context that authentically reflects how mathematics is practiced in students' lived experiences. Propose how the standard helps to promote authentic inquiry and agency.

Real-world contexts are culturally relevant when they feature intentional cultural and community inquiry and if they target social agency and action.

Consider the following grade 8 standard regarding scientific notation:

FIGURE 4.2 ● Potential task-building actions of an eighth-grade standard

Demand. The math constraint focuses on an essential idea for scientific notation and prompts nonobvious comparison between two quantities.

CCSS.MATH.CONTENT.8.EE.A.3
Use numbers expressed in the form of a single digit times an integer power of 10 to estimate very large or very small quanitities, and to express how many times as much one is than the other.

Relevance. There is opportunity to inquire how large and small quantities are expressed in community and culture (astronomy, medicine, population, wealth, nature patterns).

Agency. When we consider population and land and wealth distribution among nations, we challenge students to consider the scope of wealth inequality and how economic policy impacts population growth.

In the deconstruction of the eighth-grade standard in Figure 4.2, we see the potential for mathematical demand in fostering "nonobvious" comparison of numbers that are particularly large or small. Exploring how these numbers show up in real context to students' daily lives is particularly useful and relevant. Lastly, the standard calls for students to make determinations about these numbers upon inspection. We see that as a promising space for building agency, given a suitable context.

Based on this standard, we created the following task about national debt.

Image source: iStock.com/Dilok Klaisataporn

A country's national debt level is a measurement of how much its government owes its public creditors. For example, in December 2021 the U.S. national debt was listed at approximately $28,908,200,106,987. (www.investopedia.com/articles/economics/10/national-debt.asp)

a. Explore the national debts of three countries of similar population size to the United States, representing each debt in scientific notation. How do the national debts of these countries compare to that of the United States?

b. Research global and public debts of nations. Consider the implications of these debts. What can you say about the relationship between debt and wealth inequalities among nations? How might you or others address this issue?

In the national-debt problem, we honor the intent of having doers tackle the demand of looking at very large or small real-world numbers using scientific notation. The task is also designed to look at the problematic ways financial debt is characterized in the world. The hope is that a task like this, through its social prompt, pushes inquiry into national debt.

The additional question of community impact helps to have students make sense of this for themselves *and* as members of the global community.

In the following example, we unpack sixth-grade Common Core Math Content Standard 6.RP.A.1: Understand ratio concepts and use ratio reasoning to solve problems.

Consider the problem we adapted from a website focused on redistricting and representation:

To account for changing populations, jurisdictions redesign the maps that determine their voting districts every decade (Kennedy et al., 2016). Exploring redistricting plans is a chance to explore voter representations. Let's suppose, in a district of 50 people, voter affiliation to gray and blue political parties is roughly 60:40, as shown in Figure 4.3a.

FIGURE 4.3A • A guide to redistricting

A guide to redistricting
Three examples of how to divide 50 people into 5 districts

Let's say there is a town with 50 residents and five seats on the town council. Each district should have 10 people so that each elected official represents the same number of people—this is the concept of "one person, one vote." Of the 50 town residents, 60 percent are members of the gray party and 40 percent are members of the blue party. In a fair system, they should be able to compete for and win representation for their different views on the town council. But that depends on how the districts within the town are drawn. These maps show how districts can be drawn to facilitate equitable results or to favor one party.

50 people total:
■ 60% ■ 40%

Image Source: This material, "Redistricting and Representation: Drawing Fair Election Districts Instead of Manipulated Maps," was published by the Center for American Progress.

a. In the following diagram (Figure 4.3b), there are two possible division scenarios for this population that impact representation equity.

b. Using the diagram, draw two additional possible scenarios for voter representation that might arise. How does each of these scenarios impact voter representation equity?

c. If this town grows to 75 residents, construct a redistricting grid that represents the new population with fair representation. Discuss the assumptions that make this possible.

d. Show how each of the additional scenarios you have posed might impact the possibilities for fair voter representation.

e. Suppose that because of unplanned demographic changes, the city now calls for new redistricting proposals. Research some ways you might get involved in your community's redistricting process. Is there a particular cause you might champion?

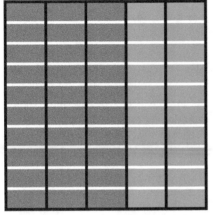
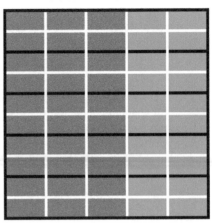
In the redistricting task, prompts are created to intentionally support students to "understand ratio concepts and use ratio reasoning to solve problems" (CCSS.MATH.CONTENT.6.RP.A.1). In examining fairness, students are further prompted to expand their understandings (remember the Culturally Relevant Mathematics Practices in Chapter 2) about redistricting. These are important issues that students may not have experience with directly but which are playing out in their communities. Tasks such as this may also have the residual effect of inspiring further conversations as students interact with community members and families. As a result, students may develop and refine positions of justice for voters.

Now, let's look at the following grade 8 Common Core Math Standard on Functions. Consider a deconstruction of this standard through the lens of the dimensions we have discussed thus far:

The standard in Figure 4.4 is not explicit about culture, but it underscores the reality teachers face in working with common standards to adapt math experiences. With some probing, it may possess opportunities for exploration of several of our dimensions for culturally relevant teaching.

—

.Demand. The opportunity to explore multiple representation in algebra; connecting symbolic, graphical, tabular, and verbal representation is a core focus for building strong understanding.

Relevance. Selecting a linear function opens up possibilities of choosing from a variety of real and imagined contexts (e.g., a community fundraising concert to save a landmark).

CCSS.MATH.CONTENT.8.F.A.2

Compare properties of two functions, each represented in a different way (algebraically, graphically, numerically in tables, or by verbal descriptions). For example, given a linear function represented by a table of values and a linear function represented by an algebraic expression, determine which functions have the greater rate of change.

Agency. Change is a powerful social topic, and looking at change rates involving economics, health, populations, and housing are possible areas for exploration.

At this point, one may be overwhelmed with decisions about content, appropriateness, and interest. The pre-work to the kind of design we are referring to involves building from (1) powerful student and family relationships, (2) deep knowledge about community and cultures, and (3) an empowerment view (versus deficit) toward students and their communities, which we will explore in later chapters. Think of this as a journey in which you can grow in competence with time and commitment. The practice of finding the opportunities in standards is an important emerging step in culturally relevant design and will undoubtedly improve with practice and earnest intention.

Through the examples we've given, you may see that the work of making standards come alive through thinking about culturally relevant task-building dimensions can be messy. What probably sticks out is that the default structure of standards seems to, at best, support cognitive demand with math that is culturally "neutral." "Neutral" is a loaded word depicting contexts that default to dominant culture. Even with "real-world" wording, there is intentional work to be done by the planner to relate and embed work around this standard as culturally relevant for their students. This is why so much of the best intended curricula we see is not neutral but is actually culturally ignorant and reflective of huge, missed opportunities. Something else that should stick out is the seemingly "messy" overlap of relevance and agency in some of our notes. This overlap makes sense when you understand that agency in mathematics can only be achieved in relation to connecting issues and challenges to what is local,

IMAGINE

Choose a national or state curriculum standard for geometry and analyze it for opportunities for cultural relevance. How does the potential in this content area compare to others? What do you notice and wonder?

ASK

What are some additional considerations for moving beyond neutral contexts and building demand, relevance, and agency into tasks?

cultural, and valued. One without the other results in a potentially inauthentic task context and almost always misses the point of embedding student culture and community.

PLANNING TASKS THAT FOSTER HOPE

Reconstructing standards in the way we have outlined is not enough to build all tasks to lead to powerful culturally affirming experiences. So far, what we have discussed seems to work well in situations where planning conditions require strict or managed adherence to curriculum standards. But increasingly in our work, we have been asked to help teachers and schools respond to important society and community "shifts" and events as they happen. In these situations, we must use our teaching to help respond positively in the moment to support students and their communities. In the section that follows, we will introduce the Hope Wheel, a powerful planning tool for selecting goals to frame tasks in a positive and affirming way. We will also share examples of how we have used this tool in our work with teachers.

RESPONDING BEYOND BLOOM

An important role of schools of education and teacher education agencies is to help teachers *unpack* curriculum standards. A common approach is to use Bloom's taxonomy as the standard for creating instructional objectives and to apply cognitive science research of developmental progressions on how children learn math. While this is helpful (for instance, knowing when a child's brain is developed enough to understand the concept of ratio), planning for culturally relevant mathematics teaching requires a deeper dive beyond standards and Bloom's progressions.

As a refresher, Bloom's taxonomy (Figure 4.5) orders six verbs of learning (Remembering, Understanding, Applying, Analyzing, Evaluating, and Creating) from recalling information (at the most basic level) to developing new ideas (at the most complex level). Although we see understanding as being multifaceted and more complex than a linear progression (a great exploration of the six facets of understanding is found in the book *Understanding by Design* by Grant Wiggins and Jay McTighe, 2001), we also believe that planning culturally relevant teaching for today's classroom means moving beyond the often spiritless frames of these classifications into a view that is more holistic and humanizing.

FIGURE 4.5 ● Bloom's taxonomy revised for 21st century learners

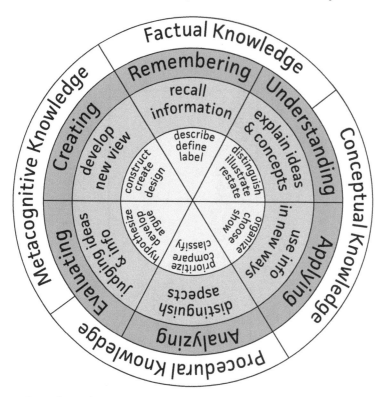

Source: Center for Teaching & Learning Excellence—The University of Utah. Wheel adapted from *Edutechnology*.

RESPONDING WITH HOPE

The Hope Wheel (Figure 4.6) was created by Dr. Lou Matthews in 2019 with the intention of supporting educators and leaders with new ways of crafting lesson learning sessions to respond to racial and social injustice, as well as social crises. The Hope Wheel is composed of six social response verbs: *Love, Protest, Restore, Create, Inspire,* and *Invest.* The verbs were drawn from themes based on notions of empowerment and what makes a "strong Black community," which includes ways to draw from and build on community wealth, community health and safety, community wisdom, community love, collective power, and justice (see Matthews, 2018).

In the same way that Bloom's taxonomy has provided verbs that teachers can use in their tasks to prompt students to think at various levels, the Hope Wheel provides teachers with verbs that can be used to plan for CRMT experiences for their students.

FIGURE 4.6 ● The Hope Wheel (www.thehopewheel.com)

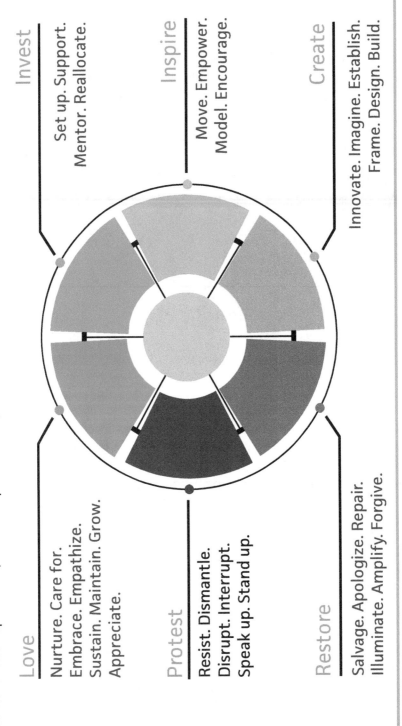

Love

Nurture. Care for.
Embrace. Empathize.
Sustain. Maintain. Grow.
Appreciate.

Protest

Resist. Dismantle.
Disrupt. Interrupt.
Speak up. Stand up.

Restore

Salvage. Apologize. Repair.
Illuminate. Amplify. Forgive.

Invest

Set up. Support.
Mentor. Reallocate.

Inspire

Move. Empower.
Model. Encourage.

Create

Innovate. Imagine. Establish.
Frame. Design. Build.

Source: Created by Lou Matthews, 2020.

online resources ↗ To view and download a full-color version of the Hope Wheel©, please visit www.loumatthews.live/hopewheel, the *Engaging With Culturally Relevant Math Tasks (Secondary)* Free Resources tab on the Corwin website, or https://bit.ly/3Lgv22E.

The Hope Wheel helps us create what we see as "hope" standards—goals and objectives reimagined for justice and cultural inquiry. With these verb categories, we want teachers to extend the process of unpacking standards and using them to design task goals. Using this information, teachers can select, adapt, and modify standards and intentions as part of the creation process.

ADAPTING CONTENT STANDARDS WITH HOPE VERBS

One approach is to select an existing content standard and then use the Hope Wheel to sharpen the focus and build out a context for relevance and agency (remember, standards are often vague in this regard). The following is an example of this approach in action, using a middle school statistics standard.

Massachusetts Curriculum Framework Standard

Statistics and Probability 8.SP.A. Investigate patterns of association in bivariate data. 1. Construct and interpret scatter plots for bivariate measurement data to investigate patterns of association between two quantities. Describe patterns such as clustering, outliers, positive or negative association, linear association, and non-linear association.

This standard requires students to solve problems using the statistical thinking process. So much of the statistical thinking process involves using data to make decisions about resources. But we can elevate this to the realm of culturally relevant teaching when we envision how students, in community, can be empowered to use mathematics as they stand up for the rights of people. Using the Hope Wheel, we can choose the Protest verb "Stand up" to sharpen this focus even further. See how we created a "hope" instructional objective by adapting the original:

<u>We</u> will <u>stand up</u> *for improved voter booth distribution in a local neighborhood of the students' choice, create a scatter plot from the city's latest report on voting booth distribution, and prepare a presentation. In their presentation, students will identify the variables and demonstrate an analysis of the graph's content.*

As you can see, this example shows how cognitively demanding math tasks can be framed so that they ask students to interact with their community in a meaningful way and empower them to take action (Protest). Also note in the example how we reframe the conversation as "We will" to denote the solidarity of the teacher with students.

Let's take a look at adapting another content standard:

CCSS.MATH.CONTENT.7.NS.A.1

Apply and extend previous understandings of addition and subtraction to add and subtract rational numbers; represent addition and subtraction on a horizontal or vertical number line diagram.

The concept of rational numbers is one of the most challenging areas students must contend with throughout elementary, middle, and high school. Many students struggle to learn rules and algorithms for fraction operations such as finding common denominators when adding and subtracting. For this reason, applying and extending understandings of rational numbers are core topics of focus for seventh-grade students. Extending how students represent rational numbers and their operations and applying these concepts to the real world ensures they can make greater connections to their own experiences.

Looking back, recall our discussion of the Culturally Relevant Math Practices (www.relevantmath.org) in Chapter 2. The CRMPs called for *expanded understandings* where children "expand understandings of mathematical concepts, algorithms, histories and cultures, to pursue solutions that matter." The phrase "solutions that matter" rings powerfully here. Hope Wheel verbs (and their synonyms) provide the means to stretch student experiences. One example of an instructional objective focused on rational numbers that meets our vision of the Hope Wheel is found embedded in a lesson on the *Citizen Math* website:

Adapted Standard/Instructional Objective:

Students order and subtract integers to explore major milestones in human history and debate whether humans are innovating faster than we can keep up with the consequences. (www.citizenmath .com/lessons/about-time)

This is an excellent example of how a teacher might use a Hope Wheel verb to adapt a standard such as this Common Core Math standard. In this particular lesson, the verb "debate" can be thought of as synonymous with the Hope Wheel verb "Protest," as it requires students to think critically and consider the implications of the pace of technological innovation as they look through history. Using positive and negative integers to represent key milestones, students can then be asked to present their findings on a vertical or horizontal number line diagram, as requested in the original standard. Expanding understandings and engaging human experience are two Culturally Relevant Mathematics Practices made possible with this focus.

Using the hope verb "Inspire," we can adapt this same Common Core math standard to provide opportunity for students to be empowered to use fraction operations to do something they all love to do—make music.

ASK

Choose a content standard from your grade level or content area. Use a Protest verb to adapt it.

Adapted Standard/Instructional Objective:

We will expand our understandings of multiplication and division of fraction operations as we explore the music that inspires our communities.

FIGURE 4.7 ● The mathematics of musical notes

Name of Note	Whole	Half	Quarter	Eighth	Sixteenth
Note Symbol	𝅝	𝅗𝅥	♩	♪	♬
Fraction of Measure	$\frac{1}{1}$	$\frac{1}{2}$	$\frac{1}{4}$	$\frac{1}{8}$	$\frac{1}{16}$
Number of notes that fit into one measure	$1=2^0$	$2=2^1$	$4=2^2$	$8=2^3$	$16=2^4$

Source: Jones and Pearson (2013).

With the instructional objective adapted from the standard, we see opportunities to create math experiences where students explore music of the community while connecting math concepts. Many students learn how to read sheet music starting around fourth grade and often don't recognize the extent of fraction operations in reading music (see Figure 4.7). This is a missed opportunity to connect math to something cherished in the "real world" of students' lives.

For example, a dotted half note (𝅗𝅥.) is a half note plus half of a half note. You can use drawings to show $\frac{1}{2}$ of $\frac{1}{2}$ or you can use fraction multiplication to find $\frac{1}{2}$ of $\frac{1}{2}$ or half of any other note. In this scenario, students might be prompted to choose and examine popular community and cultural music. After learning the notes, students can test their knowledge using fraction operations. Students will undoubtedly want to talk about songs they

IMAGINE

Choose another standard and a different hope verb. Create an instructional objective using that verb.

know and may even bring in sheet music of their favorite songs. They can learn about time signatures and discover that most popular songs are in 4/4 time, meaning there are four beats per measure (top number of the time signature) and the quarter note gets the beat (bottom number). Countless lessons on fractions can be created using music notation.

CREATING TASK GOALS FROM HOPE VERBS

Another effective way to use the Hope Wheel is to create or adapt tasks directly—that is, rather than starting with a content standard as the foundation, teachers can follow a process that starts with the Hope Wheel itself: (1) Choose a hope verb to set the intention of the task, (2) create a context that illuminates that verb, and (3) choose mathematics content to embed within this context. Note that aligning with a content standard is not always possible and may not always be a priority. We have seen teachers use the Hope Wheel in ways that envision math classroom environments beyond content. We love this!

Consider the following vignette.

VIGNETTE 9: REMIXING THE MATHEMATICS CURRICULUM

Image source: iStock.com/FatCamera

When students came back to in-person learning after the pandemic subsided, they really needed time to talk to each other. It took some time for me to engage students in the mathematics. The beauty of the moment was that as students talked, I listened. I learned a lot about what they had gone through, including learning about some of the traumatic experiences they previously had learning mathematics. I immediately told them that we would not be using the assigned textbook but instead would do real-life math. From that moment, I had buy-in from most of my middle school mathematics class. I asked them about what was going on in their lives. I then had to learn how to use that information in planning my math lessons. I would take inventory of what everyone else was doing in the district. I would do this by looking at the content in the textbook and then "remixing it to make something new." At times, I would allow my students to work with me to put together a lesson that they would find value in.

—*Mr. E. Taylor*

Mr. Taylor went on to create a lesson rooted in the Create verb. He had students use their ingenuity to make an argument to a parent about purchasing one brand of sneakers over another brand. The idea was that although one brand of sneakers was more expensive—let's say Yeezys versus Jordans because they manufacture fewer pairs of Yeezys—the Yeezy purchase would eventually yield a better investment. Students would need to make their argument by showing an understanding of using proportional relationships to solve a multistep percentage problem (CCSS.MATH.CONTENT.7.RP.A.3).

TRY THIS!

1. Choose a hope verb.

2. Then, generate a relevant context.

3. Finally, choose math content and embed within the context.

Another example of using the Hope Wheel is to engage students in a school or classroom community issue such as bullying. We might start with choosing a verb from the wheel (in this case, Restore) and creating a math task appropriate for your grade level. Consider the following objective:

Students will propose a statistical question they could ask about bullying. For example, if they are interested to know who the bullies are in their school they might ask the question, "Are the bullies in this school upper-class students?" They can collect data, choose and create an appropriate data display, and then analyze the data and report on it. For purposes of not calling out bullies by name, the data collected could be the numbers of bullies by grade level. The final step is to discuss ways of Restoring the harm done to classmates by bullies—not necessarily an endeavor in mathematics, but important, nonetheless.

IMAGINE

Now you try it! Choose a hope verb. Choose a common occurrence in your school or community. Now choose a math task that can be embedded within this real-world context.

No curriculum, standards, or wording will lead to the automatic creation of culturally relevant teaching without powerful new thinking about the nature of mathematics, who it is for, and what it can be used for.

No curriculum, standards, or wording will lead to the automatic creation of culturally relevant teaching without powerful new thinking about the nature of mathematics, who it is for, and what it can be used for. We believe that the Hope Wheel provides for such thinking. What should be taken from our use of the Hope Wheel and our deconstructing of content standards is that planning work for culturally relevant mathematics tasks begins with careful and deliberate attention.

Summary and Discussion Questions

We stated in our introduction to this chapter that planning begins with intentional goals, and then we explored how to analyze a local, state, or national content standard to find opportunities for CRMTasks. We ended the chapter with an introduction to the Hope Wheel, which, like Bloom's taxonomy, can be used to further adapt standards, using hope verbs to frame tasks in a positive and affirming way. In our next chapter, we will look at creating contexts for cultural inquiry. Before moving on, use the following questions to consider how you can use the tools and ideas presented in this chapter.

1. As you begin to put into practice the ideas presented in this book, consider the following questions when planning a CRM-Task for your classroom. What are your *intentional* goals for your task as it relates to *relevance* and *agency*? How is it based on an empowerment stance?
2. What experience—beyond the math—do you want your students to have as a result of being engaged in the task?
3. As you plan your CRMTask, which standards have you found to naturally have greater utility for creating tasks of demand, relevance, and agency?
4. As stated in this chapter, the term "real world" carries opportunities to focus on critical issues that potentially help students to exercise critical consciousness and responsiveness as citizens. What are some adjustments you need to make to your teaching methods to align with this focus?

CHAPTER 5

Creating Contexts for Cultural Inquiry

In this chapter, we will explore creating contexts for cultural inquiry. We will

- Use a cultural inquiry process to emphasize caring and belonging
- Explore student interviews to build cultural contexts
- Explore Community Walks to build cultural knowledge for contexts
- Explore using cultural literature and media to build from cultural knowledge
- Explore using cultural artifacts as a source of mathematical knowledge

It was not uncommon in later observations of Marie's class to see a mix of both traditional and nontraditional approaches to teaching, but in these early observations, this was not the case: Her method of teaching was predominantly traditional and strictly tied to the text. This meant there was usually very little room for exploration of students' ideas and strategies. She would later tell me that as her comfort level increased so did her ability to incorporate students' perspectives into the lesson. Marie shifted focus as she began "connecting" by using an illustration that she believed to be familiar to the students—customs duty and the importation of goods into Bermuda.

(Matthews, 2003, p. 75)

This conversation with Marie illustrates a journey of "letting go" of the reliance on cookie cutter ideas in order to "let in" the world of the student. In the previous chapter, we saw that standards typically provide attention to cognitive demand but offer little or vague support for creating contexts that prompt students to inquire deeply about what's valued and loved in their communities. Cognitive demand should not be the sole or privileged measure of rigor. Here, we pause and challenge you to consider how the words "rigor" and "challenge" are often synonymous but used without cultural ways of knowing. We advocate for centering relevance (task-building action 2) as a part of your design skills. This is as much a matter of the heart as it is of the head. In this chapter, we give deliberate attention to inquiring about the cultural brilliance and wisdom of children and their communities. We focus on this inquiry as the central source of math activity by exploring five approaches to building authentic contexts for tasks. We'll discuss what each of the following approaches means and explore examples where it is applied to build inquiry contexts:

- Emphasizing We Care/We Belong
- Conducting student interviews
- Conducting Community Walks
- Inquiring through media and literature
- Creating from cultural artifacts

Cognitive demand should not be the sole or privileged measure of rigor.

EMPHASIZING WE CARE/WE BELONG TO CREATE CULTURAL INQUIRY

One of the simplest ways to think about cultural inquiry-based approaches is to reflect on a common model given to teachers for promoting inquiry. In classrooms everywhere, familiar posters of "I notice, I think, I wonder" are hung as inspiration to prompt both students and teachers to open up their thinking routines to inquiry. Cultural inquiry draws from inquiry-based learning, which actively positions students at the center of the learning process.

In the inquiry process, students are given a sufficiently open-ended problem and asked, "What do you notice?" to launch their thinking about mathematical ideas. As they process and strategize, it is helpful to encourage them to communicate their noticings/wonderings. For example, in Figure 5.1

FIGURE 5.1 ● I notice, I think, I wonder

Image source: iStock.com/trait2lumiere

students might notice there are two cars in each little section of the parking garage. They might wonder how many sections fit on one floor of the garage. They might ask, Where is this garage located, and how many floors does it have? Although these noticings and wonderings might lead to students figuring out the total number of cars in the garage, the solution has no real personal connection to the students.

Another task taken from a popular middle school curriculum module asks students to scale up model cars to determine if a full-size car would fit in a garage more similar to those in homes in the students' neighborhood.

Image source: iStock.com/USGirl

(Continued)

(Continued)

Measure your model car (like Hot Wheels or a similar toy car) to the nearest tenth of an inch.

a. Convert the measurement into a full-size measurement using a 1:64 scale factor.

b. Determine if two full-scale versions of your car will fit into an 18 ft. × 20 ft. garage.

c. Create a floor plan of your two-car garage using the 1:64 scale factor. Show how your two cars will fit.

(Schrock et al., 2013, pp. 49–50)

The elements of inquiry in the problem compel students to notice comparisons between the model car and a full-size version. Students will have to consider the following: that the model car will represent a real car, the vocabulary (scale factor and floor plan), and the problem scenario (can two cars fit into a two-car garage with specific dimensions). The task of having students determine if two cars can fit is open enough to generate student creativity, curiosity, and analysis. Specifically, students will need to consider what other variables are needed to make that determination. Although this garage task may better connect to students, it does not provide students with opportunity for cultural inquiry.

Let's consider a different problem that adds an element of cultural inquiry. This task prompts students to think about the concept of exponential growth over time in a way that has them predict the speed at which algae will cover a pond. A next step could ask students to write an equation to represent the situation.

On May 12, a fast-growing species of algae was accidentally introduced to a pond in an urban park. The area of the pond that the algae covers doubles each day. If not controlled, the algae will soon cover the entire surface of the pond, depriving the fish in the pond of oxygen. At the rate it is growing, this will happen on May 24.

1. On which day is the pond halfway covered?

2. On May 18, Clare visits the park. A park caretaker mentions to her that the pond will be completely covered in less than a week. Clare thinks that the caretaker must be mistaken. Why might she find the caretaker's claim hard to believe?

3. Why do you think Claire is concerned about the algae growing so quickly in the pond? How might this affect her community?

4. What fraction of the area of the pond was covered by the algae initially, on May 12? Explain or show your reasoning.

(Illustrative Mathematics, Algebra II, Lesson 1.3: Pond in a Park)

In the two garage examples, both contexts and prompts require students to notice and wonder about patterns of similarity and changes in size and quantity. But we wish to push on your expectations for inquiry even further. We extend inquiry in the algae task by asking: Why (and how) should we care? How are we connected to the context? For example, in the algae problem, is it possible for students to wonder about the nature of environments they live in—ponds and lakes? In doing this inquiry, are we able to respond and connect to our community and each other?

FIGURE 5.2 ● Approaching cultural inquiry from a "we" perspective

In Figure 5.2, we revisit the inquiry process with the emphasis on prioritizing cultural inquiry as a "we" endeavor ("we" = teachers, students, and community). The "we" is used intentionally and forces a repositioning for teachers in how they see both community and culture. It requires us to ask first these questions: How do I feel about the *people* in front of me? How am I to show up in their community? What does the community care about? What values and aspirations are apparent in this community? A trivial or incomplete approach to asking questions of caring would focus solely on students and might only lead teachers to brainstorm a list of individual student interests, but considering student interests alone does not accomplish culturally relevant teaching.

A trivial or incomplete approach to asking questions of caring would focus solely on students and might only lead teachers to brainstorm a list of individual student interests, but considering student interests alone does not accomplish culturally relevant teaching.

We can expand our understanding of the "we" focus of cultural inquiry by considering the list of context design questions and examples in Figure 5.3.

FIGURE 5.3 ● Questions for cultural inquiry

INQUIRY ELEMENT	DESIGN QUESTIONS WE ASK FOR CULTURAL INQUIRY
We Care/We Belong	How does this context and prompt affirm how children and teachers belong and identify as part of their collective (as well as individuals)?
We Notice	How might this task focus and highlight powerful aspects of community/culture?
We Wonder	How can this task deepen how we understand ourselves, our culture, the community, and the world around us? How does this task focus on how our culture/community is valued and respected?
We Respond	How can this task model care, love, and respect for our community and culture? How can this task draw from and illuminate the beauty and wisdom of my students, our community, and culture in ways that have been hidden or ignored?

In focusing on We Care/We Belong, we are intentional about using words of care and affirmation while rejecting deficit views and incorrect or harmful ideas about who children are and what their communities value.

In focusing on We Care/We Belong, we are intentional about using words of care and affirmation while rejecting deficit views and incorrect or harmful ideas about who children are and what their communities value. In revisiting the "About Time" lesson example in the previous chapter (p. 70), we share more of the lesson plan to elaborate (Figure 5.4).

FIGURE 5.4 ● Grade 7 "About Time" lesson

How has the pace of human innovation changed over time? It took 260,000 years for humans to go from the spear to the bow-and-arrow, but only 42,000 years to go from the bow-and-arrow to the atomic bomb.

Students order and subtract integers to explore major milestones in human history and debate whether humans are innovating faster than we can keep up with the consequences.

REAL-WORLD TAKEAWAYS

· Humans have been making technological innovations throughout history—in communication, in travel, in warfare. Over time, advancements from one milestone to the next have come more and more quickly.

· Future innovations—like those of the past—will likely offer convenience and meaningful enhancements to our lives; they may also come with serious dangers. It's important for society to anticipate, consider, and discuss these impending risks.

MATH OBJECTIVES

· Model "before zero" years using negative integers
· Order and position positive and negative integers on a number line
· Find the difference between integers, including negatives

Lesson at a Glance			90 min.
Launch		Watch a 2007 commercial for the first iPhone. Identify innovations that have been significant in this lifetime and across human history.	5 min.
Part One	1	Order milestones in three categories—communication, travel, warfare—from earliest to latest.	15 min.
Part One	2	For one of the categories, arrange the milestones on a number line. Notice that significant leaps happen more quickly as time passes.	25 min.
Part Two	3	Determine the time difference between various sets of milestones, including differences between BC and BC years, AD and AD years, and BC and AD years.	30 min.
Part Two	4	Watch a video mash-up about three innovations we may see in the future: auto-translation programs, self-driving cars, and robot soldiers. Discuss potential implications for humanity.	15 min.

Source: https://www.citizenmath.com/lessons/about-time

Notice the intentionality in the "Real-World Takeaways" for student wonderings about the nature of human progress. In several prompts in the lesson, students are asked to "notice that significant leaps happen more quickly as time passes." Reflecting We Care/We Belong, students are also prompted to discuss "potential implications for humanity" (as described in Part Two—4 in the Lesson at a Glance chart in Figure 5.4).

Now, consider the following problem that highlights the We Care/We Belong cultural inquiry at the family level:

Mr. Frazer learned from his middle schoolers that they value the time they spend with their families. One student in particular was very excited to tell him about spending time with her grandparents every year during their annual family reunion. Mr. Frazer decided to use this information in the following problem instead of the original idea of going on a family trip to the Grand Canyon, which is something he does with his family but which he discovered is not an experience many of his students share or value.

Image source: iStock.com/Kali9

FIGURE 5.5 ● Family Reunion task

	OPTION 1	OPTION 2	OPTION 3
Place	Park $200	Community center $450	Banquet hall $1,200

(Continued)

(Continued)

	OPTION 1	**OPTION 2**	**OPTION 3**
Invitations	Digital $25	Basic paper $55	Premium postcards $85
Food	Potluck (bring something) $5.50/person	Hamburgers & hot dogs $7/person	Catered $18.95/person
Reunion T-shirt	DIY design $3/person	Template design $6.35/person	Personalized design $12/person
Miscellaneous (unexpected costs)	I think I have everything covered. $6/person	Hmm, am I forgetting something? $8/person	I always forget things, so I better cover myself. $10/person

You are helping to plan your family reunion, which has been happening annually for your whole life. You look forward to seeing your extended family (cousins, aunts, uncles, and grandparents) every year. You and your mom are hosting this year's reunion. You have some choices to make, but you know your budget cannot exceed $3,000. Choose one option for each budget item (Figure 5.5). Total the prices based on 50 people attending the reunion.

1. Determine your total cost. Please show your work.
2. Explain the significance of your choices.
3. At the reunion, one family member will win a special prize. If there are 22 adults and 28 children at the reunion, what is the probability that the winner will be a child?

Source: Adapted from *Black Girl MATHgic We Are Family Activity Booklet*, Issue 13, July 2020.

This problem provides students with an opportunity to explore a family event that many of Mr. Frazer's students experience and care about. By having students discuss the different traditions that take place during family gatherings, he will create opportunities for cultural inquiry. Students could discuss possible banquet locations in their community, culturally specific food items they would choose for the banquet, and meaningful T-shirt design ideas. The openness of the last item, miscellaneous, could allow for a lot of creativity in discussing activities at the family reunion. By creating this task, Mr. Frazer is providing a space of belonging as students reflect on traditions they care about while attending to the mathematics of the task.

CONDUCTING STUDENT INTERVIEWS TO BUILD FROM STUDENT CULTURE

In the following section, we share examples of how the work of building from culture might occur. In one of our courses, we asked a group of teacher candidates to reflect on ideas about how they would write culturally relevant mathematics tasks and lessons. The teachers had been learning about culturally relevant pedagogy, and to put their new knowledge into practice, they participated in an activity to learn more about an individual student. The goal was to have them consider how they would use asset-based information about the student in a mathematics lesson.

"Getting to Know You" Student Interview

(Shortened and modified from Foote et al., 2015)

Overview of Assignment

There are several purposes of this interview. The first is to find out more about the student, including student interests, activities the student engages in outside of school, and what the student identifies as activities at which they excel. You might find out, for example, what kind of activities in which the student engages in the community with their friends and family (i.e., does the student play soccer at a local park, go to a community center, shop at a particular place, etc.). The second goal is to identify places, locations, and activities in the community that are familiar to the student and to find out what they know about potential mathematical activity in those settings. These could include locations in the neighborhood immediately surrounding the school (i.e., places that are more or less in walking distance), locations/settings in the neighborhood in which the student lives (if that differs from the community surrounding the school), as well as locations/settings in the broader community with which the student is familiar. A third purpose is to find out more about the students' ideas, attitudes, and/or dispositions toward mathematics.

Conducting the Interview

Select one student from your practicum classroom who is different from you in one or more sociocultural ways (i.e., race, socioeconomic status, home language; do not select ONLY on the basis of difference in gender) AND who seems to you to struggle at least somewhat with mathematics. Conduct an interview with this student; then, in a one-page reflection introduce your student, explain why you selected this student, tell what you learned about the student, and present your ideas of how you can use the information you learned about the student to plan a mathematics lesson.

As preparation for these new teachers to write a culturally relevant lesson, in addition to conducting the student interviews, they also read scholarly articles on culturally relevant pedagogy (CRP) and teaching mathematics for social justice (TMfSJ).

ASK

What was your first experience learning about culturally relevant teaching? When did you first experience culturally relevant teaching for yourself? Describe the experience.

Many of them reported that the readings were the first time they had heard of CRP or TMfSJ. Prior to these readings, the teachers recognized that they needed to take student interest into consideration when writing lessons; however, they were unaware that culture could—and should—play a part. You should notice in the assignment that the teachers were prompted to learn about the student's activities outside of school and about activities where the student excels.

The quality of lesson ideas that resulted from the student interviews varied greatly in terms of the teacher's ability and comfort with incorporating cultural referents into a math lesson. Some teachers focused on superficial factors they learned about the student, while other teachers learned detailed information about the student to incorporate into a math lesson. The following vignette is one teacher's reflection on how they could incorporate information about a student into a mathematics lesson.

VIGNETTE 10: GETTING TO KNOW A STUDENT WHO IS DIFFERENT FROM ME

I had the pleasure of interviewing a student from my student teaching experience. Amanda is a freshman in high school who speaks English and has grown up in a very different environment than I did. Amanda grew up in an urban district in which 64% of the high school student population is minority. I chose this student because I was confident that she would be open to sharing freely. Having grown up in a suburban town, I thought it would be great to interview a student with quite a different upbringing.

After interviewing this student, I was able to learn a ton about her that I hadn't known prior when I was her student teacher. Amanda shared that she loves spending time with her family and friends, she enjoys painting, and music is really important to her. Traditionally, she and her friends walk around town, play board games, make TikToks, and go out to dinner together.

When I transitioned into some math questions, Amanda was able to provide lots of insight. She is currently in the accelerated Algebra 1 class. When I asked her who in her life uses math, she was able to point out that obviously math teachers use math all the time. In addition, she explained that, as a student, she uses math, and her sister who is a cashier has to use math every single day. Her mom also uses math when she works on paying the bills. She explained that, while we don't always recognize it, almost everyone uses math in some capacity. Amanda shared that her strongest topics in math include graphing, solving equations, and solving for variables. She shared that she struggles with fractions consistently, and this is something that she has struggled with since elementary school. In math class, she enjoys when she learns something from the teacher and gets to the point where she can do it on her own without questions. She said that math is super important because "without it, the world would be a huge mess."

After this interview, I reflected on lessons that I remembered from my student teaching experience when Amanda did well. One example was during our ratios and proportions unit. Amanda excelled and was able to share her knowledge to help her classmates. This unit was built on many student-centered lessons and error analysis. I am now able to recognize that these types of lessons were very productive for Amanda, and I would definitely use a similar structure in the future.

In this vignette, the beginning teacher is looking back to consider how she would use the information she learned about the student to support her in learning mathematics. She plans to create mathematics lessons that are student-centered and that provide students with opportunities to correct their errors on graded assignments. This is a great start for this beginning teacher. There are countless other opportunities that one could infer from the interview to plan for math lessons.

ASK

What did you learn about Amanda that could be used to plan a lesson from an asset-based perspective and that builds from the student's culture?

In the next vignette, another teacher writes about how they plan to use the student interview information to create a culturally relevant lesson.

VIGNETTE 11: GETTING TO KNOW A STUDENT WHO IS QUIET IN CLASS

The student I interviewed is a sixth grader at Lindley Street School. The student, Marley, is from an upper-middle-class family. His family includes two older sisters, a mother, and a father. At home, they only speak English. He comes from a school where minority enrollment is 35.5%, and about 40% of students receive free or reduced lunch. Overall, Lindley Street School falls below state average in mathematics proficiency, reading proficiency, and minority student enrollment. Of the 35% of minority enrollment, 24% are Hispanic. This student was selected because he struggles with math and comes from a different background than I do. This student is different from me in a few respects. One difference is gender. Also, this student has grown up with technology and has an iPad and smartphone. I did not have a laptop or cell phone until I was in high school. I also did not have access to the internet at home growing up. Socioeconomic status is also a difference. Growing up, I came from a working-class family. I also had a large family with three sisters, my mom, and grandparents. When I was in high school, our school implemented a remedial learning hour. Some similarities are that we come from English-only households, have more than one sister, and both our schools fell below state averages in proficiency in general.

Through the interview, I learned much more about the student than I expected. In class, he is quiet and does not often volunteer to answer questions. When we work together during math time, he is cautious to move on from a problem until he is sure he got the current one correct. Some things Marley likes to do are go to the high school track to run, play outdoors with his family, and go on vacations to Lake George. He also said his family likes to cook and clean together. When it comes to math, Marley says he is good at basic arithmetic but still struggles with the 7 times tables. Algebra is another struggle that he would like to overcome even though he knows that he will get more practice in seventh grade. He believes that being good at math means that you can solve problems fast and without hesitation. He thinks the more minutes it takes to solve a problem, the worse you are at it. An important thing to note is that he thinks it is hard for some people to learn math because they do not get enough time. He even used himself as an example; he struggles at math, but when he is given more time, he can get it.

When asked where he sees math in the community, Marley thought of high school students doing math, cashiers handling money at the grocery store, and telling time. He also thinks it is important to know math because when you grow up, you'll need to know it for monetary purposes. The information gathered in this interview could help shape a lesson plan by incorporating things the student is interested in or thinks are important. Math problems that include decimals and incorporate team sports or running may interest him. Because many stores and restaurants like DQ and McDonalds are present in the community and Marley thinks money is very important, I could create problems to incorporate the cost of items or budgets. To expand on his abilities, I think it would be important to plan for math problems that show other types of math adults do that are not monetary. I also think many students would benefit from a math talk and/or math problems that take time to solve so that they can realize that speed is not equivalent to "being smart" or mathematical ability. I could also incorporate probability with card games, and doubling or tripling recipes can incorporate multiplying and dividing fractions. Overall, it is important to find some way to connect the students with math so that it is not just rote memorization and procedure.

ASK

Compare Vignettes 10 and 11. How are the teachers' approaches to using student interview information similar and/or different? What recommendations would you provide to each teacher?

Going back to Amanda, the student highlighted in Vignette 10, the teacher was asked to consider planning a lesson from an asset-based perspective. Did the teacher consider that the student enjoys painting and music? Math connections to painting and similar artistic endeavors include using ratio and proportion for scale and also transformations and patterns seen in visual art. Music is full of the meaning of fractions and fraction operations. In some music, you could also see transformations happening (usually a translation of the musical notes). There are lots of patterns in music as well—think about the rhythm of the music. Amanda also talks about board games, which are chock full of math. Think about Dominoes, Mancala, and any board game that involves using number cubes to advance spaces and keeping score. Think about Monopoly and how some of the spaces involve taking rent and paying interest. When Amanda and her friends go to dinner, we hope they know how to figure out the tip—that is, if it isn't already listed on the bill. If Amanda and her friends like TikTok so much, maybe they would like to be assessed by creating a TikTok video to teach their friends a math concept they've learned. These are just a few ideas that the teacher could use to make richer connections to Amanda. It is interesting that the teacher says that Amanda struggles with fractions but did very well with ratios and proportions. How might the teacher help Amanda make a connection between these concepts?

In Vignette 11, it was clear that the teacher picked up on a very important part of teaching mathematics. They wanted to make it clear to their students that faster in math does not mean smarter in math. Trying to find opportunities for students to persevere and solve problems will help them to understand that some mathematics problems take time. Creating math talks is a great way to orchestrate discourse about the mathematics in a way that can help students see that math is more than the answer you get. By starting with contexts that students care about and then incorporating elements of We Notice/We Wonder (via Number Talks or other instructional strategy), the teacher can create a classroom culture where students want to Respond. There is value in their response because it is meaningful to them.

Other information that teachers used from student interviews included sports (i.e., basketball, football, gymnastics, soccer), video games and toys (i.e., Minecraft, Fortnite©, Legos©, superheroes, etc.), creative arts (i.e., drawing, singing, dancing), outside activities (i.e., trampoline park, playing tag with siblings and friends), reading, playing with animals, and other student interests. We should be reminded here that focusing on students' interests alone does not accomplish culturally relevant teaching; however, it is a starting point for these beginning teachers.

CONDUCTING COMMUNITY WALKS TO BUILD COMMUNITY KNOWLEDGE

Another strategy for learning about students is a Community Walk, which is a highly effective strategy for building from community and cultural knowledge and wisdom. We talked about this briefly in Chapter 1 and offered the Community Walk Checklist (Figure 1.3) as a tool to help you notice the differences and similarities between your school's community and the one in which you may live. We will now dive deeper into the rich possibilities of conducting a Community Walk.

An important activity for culturally relevant mathematics teaching is *designing mathematics contexts, prompts, and inquiry from culture and community sources*. The Community Walk assignment is a great way to move beyond learning about students' interests and connect learning to a more meaningful understanding of their lived experiences. Exploring community funds of knowledge (FoK) also provides greater opportunity to address the critical aspect of culturally relevant pedagogy in math lessons.

Community Walk Assignment

1. Visit one or more locations in the community surrounding your school. It is important that you are willing to walk off the school grounds. Select locations that are familiar to students (i.e., places that draw families in the community, social hubs).

2. During your visit, look for and document evidence of mathematics. If possible, talk to individuals who work/play/shop in the setting about how they use mathematics. Take/draw pictures and field notes. Identify how each picture or experience you document provides evidence of mathematics. During your visit, refrain from making judgments about the neighborhood. The goal of the Community Walk is to learn from the community and identify resources for future lesson planning. It is also a time for you to confront stereotypes or assumptions you may have.

3. If you have the opportunity, show students from your field site your photographs and have them tell you what they know about these places and, if relevant, what they (or their family) do at these places (especially if it involves mathematics). You will be amazed at how much more they will share with your photos in hand!

Teachers were given this assignment in an effort for them to both connect to their students' community and learn about the various ways mathematics is used in the community. This is to help students see that math is all around them and that people in their community are doers of mathematics. Vignette 12 and Vignette 13 show examples of two Community Walks conducted by teachers and their different responses to the visits.

VIGNETTE 12: COMMUNITY WALK: GETTING TO KNOW THE TOWN WHERE STUDENTS LIVE

My field placement this semester is at The STEM Academy in the town of Rockland. For my Community Walk assignment, I wanted to visit a location that many of the students are familiar with and have gone to more than once. I looked up many of the different parks, stores, shops, and restaurants that call Rockland home and came across an ice cream shop known as "Scoops, Sprinkles and Smiles." When asked how they use mathematics during their shifts at this shop, the employees replied that mathematics comes into play when they are ringing out customers and when they are measuring ingredients. Since they have a variety of items on their menu, they use many different forms of measuring instruments, especially when making their famous shakes and cakes. When you first walk into the shop, you notice the bright colors that the walls are painted and large plastic sweets hung on the walls throughout, such as candy and bowls of ice cream. It is very inviting for children and catches your eye when driving by because of its bright outdoor appearance as well. Incorporating this location into a classroom mathematics lesson is very realistic and would keep the students engaged because it is a place that they look forward to visiting and can envision in their mind. This could be made into a lesson for sixth graders that are working on combinations in probability, decimal operations for counting money and giving change, and ratio and proportions for adjusting recipes or knowing the amount of ice cream needed for larger parties. A sample problem can be to create an ice cream cone using the different flavors provided at this location and the different prices per scoop that they charge—for example: "You are waiting on a dad with his three children. The dad wants two scoops of vanilla ice cream in a cup. The children each want a four-scoop cone. How much would it cost in total for them to get 3 scoops of chocolate chip ice cream and 1 scoop of strawberry ice cream if one scoop of chocolate chip ice cream costs $1.00 and one scoop of strawberry and vanilla each cost $0.90? Show how you reached your answer."

IMPROVE

Vignette 12 is a great first try at accessing cultural knowledge and wisdom. What could you do to incorporate a critical stance using the information in the vignette? What are additional questions you have and might research about the community?

For example, looking back at Figure 5.3 we could ask the following question to help us better utilize the information gathered from the previous Community Walk: How can this task model care, love, and respect for our community and culture?

The next vignette is a Community Walk activity that delves a little deeper into a community issue by incorporating critical components for students to consider.

VIGNETTE 13: COMMUNITY WALK TO THE SUPERMARKET

Image source: iStock.com/Stevegeer

I visited various locations in the community surrounding Marin School. One of the locations that I took a picture of was called La Fiesta Food Mart. From researching online, I learned that the market is based on Hispanic culture and also sells take-out food that is cooked Mexican style. This market is quite small but is an important part of the community because there is a large Hispanic population within the surrounding community of the school. This market provides evidence of mathematics because in order to obtain the goods within the market, one must have the appropriate amount of money to be able to make a purchase.

As I mentioned before, the supermarket is quite small and the parking lot can barely fit three cars. The aisles are very narrow, such that only one person at a time can fit in the aisle. Students can conduct an investigation comparing this smaller market to larger supermarket chains like HEB©. They might consider the size of the building and parking lots, advertising costs, costs of items, and so on. To carry out this investigation, students would need to determine the area of the La Fiesta and HEB buildings and parking lots. Students would also determine items that are sold in both stores but are different prices. From comparing prices of the same items, students would make comparisons as to which store has higher prices.

From the data that the students collected, they can determine which store they think most people in the community would want to go to and why. They could also discuss other factors that might affect the store that customers choose to shop. One of the other factors that students could investigate is that both stores sell prepared food. For example, La Fiesta sells Mexican rice, refried beans, and various meats for take-out, while HEB has a cafe where people can buy coffee and various foods to consume within the store. The students could compare the prices on the menus and the number of options on the menu for customers to choose from, which may lead to a customer being more inclined to go to one store over the other.

Although both Community Walk scenarios involve money, Vignette 13 introduces a critical component by having students compare prices and menu options as well as discussing why community members might choose one store over the other. Students might recognize that their families patronize the smaller local store because it carries more traditional foods their family likes or they know the owners or even because of proximity to their homes. In that case, the idea is that bigger isn't always better. In Vignette 13, we answer the question from Figure 5.3: How does this task focus on how our culture/community is valued and respected? In small communities, local businesses are valued because they tend to engage with the community on a local and more personal level than the larger chain stores.

USING LITERATURE AND MEDIA TO BUILD CULTURALLY RELEVANT MATHEMATICS TASKS

Literature and media are great platforms for inspiring the building of culturally relevant mathematics tasks and for affirming the wisdom of students and their communities. The power of story and narrative are essential elements of cultural inquiry. Stories, both fiction and nonfiction, carry the histories, complexities, and inspiration of ourselves and our community. We extend our conversation about the use of literature in cultural inquiry to include other media forms such as social media, podcasts, music, poetry, comic books, and the like (see Resources) because of their prevalence in adolescent and teen life.

There are many benefits to using literature and media to make connections to mathematics. The premise of this strategy is that social and cultural media forms can be used to form the basis of task creation and adaptation. Narrative texts contain important background information that can form the basis of culturally and community-driven mathematics contexts and prompts, and fiction in particular has the power to create emotional connections and inspire empathy in the reader.

For example, the book *Take Back the Block* (Figure 5.6) by Chrystal D. Giles (2021) gives an account of an 11-year-old boy who learns about community activism to save his neighborhood from gentrification. He participates in many protest marches with his activist mom, who tries to explain why they should care about others in their community. Today, they are marching for the tenants who had to move out of their building that was demolished to make room for a new high-rise condominium. Gentrification in urban cities is a practice that is all too common today and robs the displaced residents of their history and heritage. At first

IMAGINE

Create another mathematics context and prompt to match the potential of the context offered in *Take Back the Block*.

glance, we see a book geared at fifth or sixth grade, based on the age of the main character. The story, however, lends itself to discussions about complex issues such as gentrification, which can be appropriate for older students in the secondary education space. We will expand on using social issues like gentrification as a basis for mathematics inquiry in the next chapter.

As the community marches together to save their city from further gentrification, community features are affirmed and relationships of solidarity forged. Using this backdrop for task creation centers cultural inquiry in community wisdom and acceptance. Powerful cultural inquiry cannot be crafted with deficit thinking.

FIGURE 5.6 ● *Take Back the Block* book cover

Source: Take Back the Block by Chrystal D. Giles: 9780593175200 | PenguinRandomHouse.com

---

Powerful cultural inquiry cannot be crafted with deficit thinking.

In addition to providing a cultural context and quite possibly a cultural prompt, we challenge ourselves to ask what an appropriate mathematics context and prompt might be. The vacant lot after the demolition provides opportunity to explore area and perimeter, size and shape. For example, a sixth-grade task focused on "Solve real-world and mathematical problems involving area, surface area, and volume" (CCSS.MATH. CONTENT.6.G.A.1) might have students create a proposal for a variety of "creatively shaped" garden lots and be challenged to compute and compare the areas and perimeters of garden spaces in order to maximize the development of a fixed space.

How do you choose literature and media for mathematics tasks? For this, we revisit our table of questions for cultural inquiry offered earlier in the chapter (Figure 5.3). Adopted for text and media, we offer these questions for you to ask:

- How does this text/media affirm how children and teachers belong and identify as part of their collective (as well as individuals)?

- How might this text/media focus and highlight powerful aspects of community/culture?

- How can this text/media deepen how we understand ourselves, our culture, the community, and the world around us? How does this text/media focus on how our culture/community is valued and respected?

- How can this text/media model care, love, and respect for our community and culture?

- How can this text/media draw from and illuminate the beauty and wisdom of my students, our community, and culture in ways that have been hidden or ignored?

REFLECT

What does the literature/media you currently use to promote cultural inquiry for your school/class community look like? How might you assess that literature/media using our questions of cultural inquiry?

In our work in Black communities, for example, we find that literature focused on themes of Black love, health, wealth, power, safety, and wisdom offers great contexts for affirmation and inspiration. In Figure 5.7, we offer some examples of cultural literature/media, suggest some inquiry ideas that examine elements of culture and community, and provide possible math ideas using the Hope Wheel.

FIGURE 5.7 ● Connections between selected literature, media, and cultural inquiry

TEXT/MEDIA	POSSIBLE THEMES FOR CULTURAL INQUIRY	POSSIBLE MATH IDEAS USING HOPE WHEEL
Harvesting Hope: The Story of Cesar Chavez by Kathleen Krull	History of Mexican American social movements, migrant farm workers	Students appreciate and embrace the life of Cesar Chavez as they explore the wealth contribution of migrant farm workers to the economy.
Black Panther	A marvel fantasy movie featuring Black excellence themes of love, strength, and wisdom	Students imagine empowered futures for the Black community as they examine opportunities for cooperative economics.
Hula-Hoopin' Queen by Thelma Lynne Godin	Hula hooping is a time-honored tradition in the Black urban neighborhood.	Students embrace the importance of family, intergenerational ties, and community as they calculate an appropriate budget for Miz Adeline's community birthday party.

TEXT/MEDIA	POSSIBLE THEMES FOR CULTURAL INQUIRY	POSSIBLE MATH IDEAS USING HOPE WHEEL
The Arabic Quilt: An Immigrant Story by Aya Khahil	A girl whose family emigrated from Egypt to the United States shares her Arabic culture with her classmates.	Students appreciate and honor language and traditions as they create a symmetrical quilt using quilt squares with their names written in Arabic.
When We Love Someone We Sing to Them by Ernesto Javier Martinez	A story of a boy's multiple identities brings pride to his Mexican heritage and inclusion to the LGBTQ community.	Students embrace multiple identities and groups as they use music theory and fractions to write love songs.
If You Lived During the Plimoth Thanksgiving by Chris Newell	A historical account of the feast at Plimoth between the English colonists and the Wampanoag people	Students illuminate the resilience of Indigenous people of Massachusetts and in their local communities as they explore exponential growth through the spread of diseases that were similar to the COVID-19 pandemic.

You might be reminded of some favorite books that you've used in the past to make connections between mathematics and literature. These are books that we already have in our classrooms and school libraries. Many of our old favorites, however, were not very diverse and oftentimes depicted people of color and more specifically Black people in deficit terms. The books we offer in Figure 5.7 provide some broadening of the stories we have to choose from today. These stories highlight the strength and resilience of diverse people in the United States and beyond. In addition, the stories offer more diverse contexts to create cultural inquiry in mathematics tasks.

For example, *If You Lived During the Plimoth Thanksgiving* tells the story of the arrival of the Pilgrims on the *Mayflower* from the historical perspectives of both the English settlers and the Indigenous people from the Wampanoag territory. They were skeptical of those arriving on ships due to past bad experiences, such as The Great Dying of 1616–1619 when the people of Patuxet died from the diseases brought by the people in ships. Patuxet was a Wampanoag village area where the Pilgrims settled. The world can relate to a pandemic event that causes an enormous amount of loss of life, which can be mathematized by using an exponential growth model. However, it can help students not only understand how fast exponential growth can occur but also have a concrete application to which they can relate. If someone is infected with a disease and can infect 3 other people per day, and each of those people can infect 3 other people per day, in how many days would it take for the entire community to be infected if it is not contained? A teacher could use the population of their school, city, state, and so on to pose the question to the class.

USING CULTURAL ARTIFACTS AS A SOURCE OF MATHEMATICAL KNOWLEDGE

Another approach to creating mathematics tasks from culture is in finding a cultural artifact or tradition and generating inquiry around whether this notion is currently useful, particularly in thinking about culture across local contexts. An example is given in Figure 5.8a, based on the Ishango bone, discovered in the present-day Democratic Republic of the Congo, believed to be 25,000 years old and widely considered to be the second-oldest mathematics artifact in the world.

FIGURE 5.8A ● Mathematical treasure: Ishango bone*

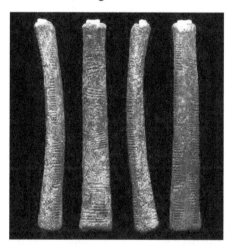

*See Resources, page 156: *Mathematicians of the African Diaspora.*

Task

Students examine the Ishango bone, the second-oldest math artifact in the world, discovered in the Democratic Republic of the Congo. As they explore the bone through pictures and video in groups, they are asked to imagine the possibilities of what it could have been used for. Students are then asked to explore and discuss the many things African and African American people have created in mathematics and are challenged to discover more "hidden figures." Students can also brainstorm common community activities involving objects that might need measuring or counting and to "create" a community bone to measure/count something they love.

This example is one of cultural inquiry, but it goes further in focusing on the contribution of African culture to mathematics. Similar tasks could be created around the many examples available of Indigenous and ancestral mathematics (consider the Peruvian quipu and the Chinese abacus). This focus stands in contrast to traditional mathematics emphasis that does not take into account the contributions of non-European communities to mathematics. We see this as an empowerment notion and a way to affirm the value of Black, Indigenous, and other non-white cultures in mathematics creation. In the Ishango bone example, the task tackles an important cognitive focus of most high school math expectations (exponential growth, growth rate, and doubling time). But perhaps more importantly, the task opens the door to conversation and probing around the exclusion of non-European knowledge in mathematics. By examining the history and relevance of the Ishango bone, students can begin to unravel a hidden, inclusive, and more expansive history of mathematics.

FIGURE 5.8B ● Notches on Ishango bone*

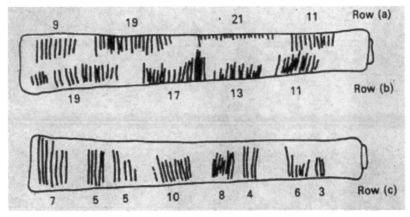

*See Resources, page 156: *Mathematicians of the African Diaspora*.

Taking a closer look at the Ishango bone, archaeologists found groups of notches in 3 columns (Figure 5.8b). A possible pattern for the first row of numbers is 10 – 1, 20 – 1, 20 + 1, and 10 + 1. What is the significance of 10? What is another possible pattern for the first row? At first glance, the number patterns on the Ishango bone might seem pretty basic or random, even. However, when we consider the era of the bone (circa 17,500 BCE) we must ask ourselves, who are these people who created a number system using "base ten," prime numbers, and possibly doubling—all of this *before* paper and pencil were invented and *before* formal schooling. Who are the children in today's classrooms who need to learn about the complex thinking that was emerging in African nations in addition to Egypt? The answer is certainly African American children, but in essence *all* children benefit from learning about the contributions of all people to mathematics. This helps us to answer the cultural inquiry question in Figure 5.3: How can this task draw from and illuminate the beauty and wisdom of my students, our community, and culture in ways that have been hidden or ignored?

Summary and Discussion Questions

In this chapter, we looked at cultural inquiry by attending to students' culture and community as a foundational basis for creating mathematics tasks. We moved away from the individual "I" to a space that embraces our collective community of "we." This process is multifaceted, with many factors to consider in this We Care/We Belong approach. To assist you in the process, we shared stories of several teachers' experiences with interviewing students and walking the community to learn about their students, which are both effective strategies to help teachers form authentic relationships with students. We also explored how using literature and other media can enhance a teacher's approach to teaching mathematics that inspires connection and affirmation in their students. In addition, investigating cultural artifacts and ancestral mathematical knowledge helped these teachers to expand the history of mathematics. With some inquiry of their own, teachers can deepen their understanding of their students' lived experiences and funds of knowledge as a resource for their teaching, shifting their focus from the mathematical complexity component of cultural inquiry to the cultural complexity of the mathematics tasks they create. Before moving to the next chapter where we will provide a process for using the cultural inquiry model to design mathematics tasks that attend to cultural complexity, consider the following questions:

1. Conducting a student interview is a good way to begin to understand students' lived experiences. When developing your questions, how can you go beyond superficial ideas about their culture and community to affirm them (We Belong)? What kinds of questions can you ask or what topics can you choose to accomplish this? Why? What powerful aspects of community/culture could you highlight with tasks taken from that topic (We Notice)?

2. We suggested taking a Community Walk to build from community and cultural knowledge and wisdom. How can you use this acquired knowledge to deepen what you understand about your students and the community/culture around them (We Think)?

3. What is valued and respected in your students' culture/community (We Think)? What media, literature, cultural artifacts, or other approaches can you use to model care, love, and respect to mine what has been ignored and illuminate what has been hidden in your students and/or in their culture and community (We Respond)?

CHAPTER 6

Creating Contexts for Empathy, Agency, and Action

In this chapter, we will

- Clarify how we prioritize empathy, agency, and action
- Explore how social justice standards can guide task creation
- Examine empathy building as the focus of design
- Promote agency and action for personal and collective empowerment
- Examine creating prompts from media and current issues

I have tried a social justice unit in my own classroom, but I did not fully commit. I was nervous with my students' reactions to the unit of study. I know that social justice units should make students feel empowered to make a change by learning essential information. However, I am nervous that once they learn about the topic, they will feel as though they can't make a change and are stuck where they are.

—Michelle, 2018

W e now tackle our most urgent guidance for task building: creating contexts and prompts that empower
students and their teachers to engage in the work of
collective action for justice. As stated throughout this book, we
believe all students deserve and want to learn mathematics in
ways that shape their lives and the lives of those around them,
and we think all teachers are capable of making this a reality.
Michelle, one of our colleagues, shares an example of the kinds
of things many teachers ponder when they teach to empower:
They wonder what this looks like, if they know enough, whether
the "mathematics" can fit. These are all design questions. On
top of that, they are concerned about how students, and others,
will respond.

In Chapter 3, we introduced the third of our three task-building actions for culturally relevant mathematics tasks: targeting
agency and action. We believe empathy is an inherent attribute
of those targets and will include it here as we explore this action
further. With this action, we attend to how task design (including intent, contexts, and prompts) is crafted to push students to
respond to the world and issues around them. In this chapter,
we ask you to consider how agency is targeted in the development and adaptation of mathematics tasks. We use words like
empathy, social justice, and collective action in the process,
while also understanding that your experiences as a teacher
of mathematics may not have involved these words. We
offer four approaches for mathematical task building to
nurture empathy, agency, and action:

- Selecting social justice standards to guide
  task design

- Creating contexts for building empathy

- Creating contexts promoting agency and action
  through personal and collective empowerment

- Creating prompts from media for responding in
  solidarity to current issues

WHEN WE SAY EMPATHY, AGENCY, AND ACTION

We use *empathy*, *agency*, and *action* to refer to how people are
able to see and use mathematics as a means of empathizing
and pursuing justice, equity, and collective action in their communities and in the world. We believe it is not only possible but
also necessary that teachers design appropriate contexts and
prompts promoting these qualities. Agency is a complex term,

Demand

Relevance

Agency

IMAGINE

Describe how each of these terms (i.e., empathy, agency, action) show up—or don't show up—in the current ways you use math tasks. How might that shift with intentional planning?

so let's take some time to be transparent about how we are using it for practice.

First, we reject deficit thinking, language, and approaches in our work to support agency, and we see ourselves as advocates, allies, and members of the communities of students we teach. Culturally relevant teaching emphasizes solidarity. We want you to see "them" in strengths-based and empowering ways as you create/adapt mathematics tasks. Doing this means paying particularly close attention to language, stereotypes, and "fix-them" approaches to context building, which we'll explore further in the coming sections.

Second, we prioritize *both* community/collective action and personal empowerment. We see the teacher as working in solidarity with communities, not merely as a facilitator of one-on-one experiences; *every* student is a proxy for the collective, representing both themselves and their community at the same time. Ignoring collective belonging and action ignores the essence of culturally relevant teaching (as opposed to personal or individually relevant teaching notions) and social justice aims.

ASK

What are examples of deficit language and thinking about people and groups? In what ways can we use language and context for solidarity with the communities we teach?

Think of agency as people being able to live a life where justice, equality, and thriving are prioritized. In the collective sense, we always mean Fighting/Standing/Speaking for Justice (remember the Culturally Relevant Mathematics Practices in Chapter 2) as fighting for "people." In our communities, we see this as exploring how racial and social equity can be better understood and addressed with and through mathematics.

We believe it is not only possible but also necessary that teachers design appropriate contexts and prompts promoting action and empathy.

SELECTING SOCIAL JUSTICE STANDARDS TO GUIDE TASK DESIGN

We see so many teachers struggle in isolation with ethical questions and their discomfort in tackling challenging—but necessary—areas of human experience. Because of this, we offer that teachers absolutely can use available standards to guide task creation. There are growing resources and curricula that can be used to frame the areas and scope for creating contexts and prompts that target agency and action. One critical source of inspiration and guidance for our work is the *Learning for Justice Standards for Social Justice* (www.learningforjustice .org). The *Learning for Justice* site, operated by the Southern Poverty Law Center, features 20 anchor standards covering four domains: identity, diversity, justice, and action. Each of the four domains is designed to assist school districts with a systemic approach to antibias, social justice, and civil rights education. In addition, the site provides excellent guidance on several topic areas such as race and ethnicity, religion, ability, class, immigration, gender and sexual identity, bullying and bias, and rights and activism.

While we strongly suggest taking the time to read through and reflect on the full list of standards, we have selected a few in particular that we feel are especially useful in exploring empathy, agency, and action for task creation in mathematics:

> *Students will recognize traits of the dominant culture, their home culture and other cultures and understand how they negotiate their own identity in multiple spaces. (Identity Anchor Standard 5)*

> *Students will examine diversity in social, cultural, political and historical contexts rather than in ways that are superficial or oversimplified. (Diversity Anchor Standard 10)*

> *Students will analyze the harmful impact of bias and injustice on the world, historically and today. (Justice Anchor Standard 13)*

> *Students will express empathy when people are excluded or mistreated because of their identities and concern when they themselves experience bias. (Action Anchor Standard 16)*

> *Students will plan and carry out collective action against bias and injustice in the world and will evaluate what strategies are most effective. (Action Anchor Standard 20)*

As an example, consider the case of Mr. Cook:

Mr. Cook will have students "examine diversity in social, cultural, political and historical contexts rather than in ways that are superficial or oversimplified" (Diversity Anchor Standard 10). He knows that students may not be familiar with the history of the Chinese laborers who were instrumental in building America's first transcontinental railroad in the mid-1800s. He develops the Railroad Workers task to achieve the education outcome of Diversity Anchor Standard 10.

Chinese Railroad Workers Project Task

Approximately 15,000 to 20,000 Chinese immigrants made major contributions, which have been largely ignored by history, to the construction of the transcontinental railroad. According to the Chinese Railroad Workers Project, Central Pacific started with a crew of 21 Chinese workers in January 1864. Chinese workers hired in 1864 were paid $26 a month, working 6 days a week.

Today's value of the wages earned by the workers can be calculated using the consumer price index (CPI) and is given by the formula (Present CPI/Past CPI) * Past money value = Today's value.

Find the today value of the yearly income in 1864 paid to a worker by researching the latest CPI data. How does the current wage value compare to wages of jobs you know? What does it say about the nature of the work completed in 1864? How should we acknowledge this contribution, today?

BUILDING EMPATHY

When students and teachers empathize, they are in a position to take action from a place of authenticity and caring. Tasks that target empathy provide prompts where students Expand Understandings (remember the Culturally Relevant Mathematics Practice in Chapter 2) of others, of communities, and "hidden" stories. The Action Anchor Standard 16 advocates that students "express empathy when people are excluded or mistreated because of their identities and concern when they themselves experience bias." For example, consider how one teacher desired to have her Algebra I students become more aware of the issue of homelessness, explore collective actions, and develop empathy for persons experiencing homelessness in their community. In response, she planned a mathematics activity she believed would increase her students' awareness of homelessness within their community.

The lesson shown in Figure 6.1a (that was featured on www.citizenmath.com) engages students in addressing the issue of homelessness. The instruction intention of the lesson is "students interpret linear equations and trend lines to describe how median income, average rent, and rates of homelessness have changed in the past two decades in various U.S. cities and discuss what they can do to aid people experiencing homelessness in their communities."

FIGURE 6.1A ● Seeking Shelter task

What factors influence homelessness in a city? Local leaders want to recruit high-paying jobs and to ensure their communities remain affordable to the people living there, and these goals can present a challenge.

In this lesson, students interpret linear equations and trend lines to describe how median income, average rent, and rates of homelessness have changed in the past two decades in various U.S. cities and discuss what they can do to aid people experiencing homelessness in their communities.

REAL-WORLD TAKEAWAYS

· In cities like New York, Los Angeles, and Seattle, average incomes have risen over time. As incomes have risen, so have rents.

· As rents rise, some people are no longer able to afford their homes and become homeless.

· Local leaders face a challenge in recruiting high-paying jobs while ensuring their areas remain affordable to the less well-off.

MATH OBJECTIVES

· Describe a line of best fit as a line which is drawn through data points to show a long-term trend
· Interpret a linear equation in a real-world contex'

Source: https://www.citizenmath.com/lessons/seeking-shelter

In one of the tasks associated with the lessons, students are prompted to analyze particular graphs depicting homelessness across the United States. The task involves students using data and linear models to explore this issue (which is aligned with Common Core State Standard CCSS.MATH.CONTENT.HSS.ID.A.3). Here, they focus on shape, center, and spread in the context of homelessness, making sense of extreme data points.

IMAGINE

Think about how your students might react to graphing similar data from their own neighborhood. What questions might they ask?

FIGURE 6.1B ● Seeking Shelter task (part 2)
Part Two: Moonlight Sleeping

Across the United States, more than 500,000 people are experiencing homelessness at any given moment. Many had homes but lost them when they could no longer afford the rent. Watch the video about some of these people.

Analyze the graphs below describing homelessness in Los Angeles and explain what they tell you. Based on this, if you sketched a graph of LA's unhoused population versus the median income, what do you expect it to look like?

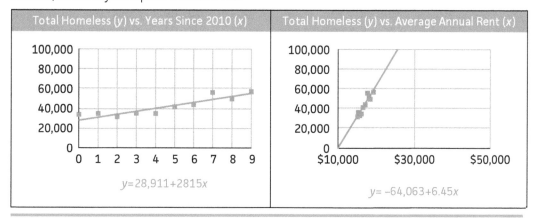

Total Homeless (y) vs. Years Since 2010 (x)

$y = 28{,}911 + 2815x$

Total Homeless (y) vs. Average Annual Rent (x)

$y = -64{,}063 + 6.45x$

PROMOTING AGENCY AND ACTION THROUGH PERSONAL AND COLLECTIVE EMPOWERMENT

A direct way to frame agency in tasks is to plan problem contexts and prompts to focus on empowering students personally. One of the most powerful elements of culturally relevant teaching lies in how it empowers teachers to work in, with, and for the communities they teach. When students possess a critical consciousness about the world around them, they are empowered to use knowledge to engage with empathy to create solutions for a just society.

When students use mathematics to solve problems in their own lives and the lives of people they care about, they develop agency and take action. Helping students understand their bodies, build positive relationships, and consider safety and growth are likely already emphasized in many places in the current curriculum. Sometimes, teachers see this as an opportunity for students to select the things that interest them, and while this approach has value, we believe this to be a great place to build and go even deeper.

When students use mathematics to solve problems in their own lives and the lives of people they care about, they develop agency and take action.

Several of the *Learning for Justice* standards talk about the challenge of taking action. More than *learning about* a community, taking action challenges us to *stand for* community. Consider Action Anchor Standard 20: *Students will plan and carry out collective action against bias and injustice in the world and will evaluate what strategies are most effective.* For example, imagine that a community of which you are a member is concerned about a building in a historically Black neighborhood that is at risk of being lost to gentrification. Let's also assume that this building is an important landmark and resource for the community of the students you teach. Creating a task like the Gentrification Response task that involves students as members of the community "response" is a powerful action for supporting agency.

The Gentrification Response task has students conduct a spatial analysis of the kinds of graphs that are used to describe how a population group is located historically. We like that students doing the problem will have to look at shapes and space and figure out estimated areas of regular and nonregular objects and spaces (CCSS.MATH.CONTENT.HSG.MG.A.2). Differing estimates will provide a basis for rich discourse, while checking

Gentrification Response Task

Washington, D.C., features one of the heaviest gentrification rates with its historic Black resident populations. How can we support residents in stemming the impact of gentrification efforts? Using the graphs drawn from the two censuses (Figure 6.2), create a method for analyzing the spatial dots to find an estimate for the change in Black residents per block group depicted. Using the method, estimate the extent of change for Black residents. How might this compare to other jurisdictions you are familiar with?

FIGURE 6.2 ● Washington, D.C., gentrification map

Fewer blacks in the District
New Census data shows the District continued to lose black residents over the last 20 years.

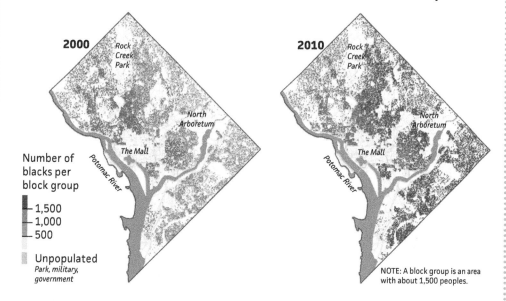

Source: Race and ethnicity map of Washington, D.C. with 2000 Census Data (2011). No changes made. https://commons.wikimedia.org/wiki/File:Race_and_ethnicity_map_of_Washington,_D.C..png , CC BY-SA 2.0, https://creativecommons.org/licenses/by-sa/2.0/deed.en; Race and ethnicity in Washington , D.C. 2010 (2011). No changes made. https://commons.wikimedia.org/wiki/File:Race_and_ethnicity_in_Washington,_D.C._2010.png, CC By-SA 2.0, https://creativecommons.org/licenses/by-sa/2.0/deed.en

these answers against reported narratives will help students to make stronger connections.

> *More than* learning about a *community, taking action challenges us to* stand for *community.*

In the following refined task, we use our focus on action to adapt existing tasks. Take a look at how we start with an original task from a secondary text and use it to create a geometry task focused on neighborhood clean-up.

Original Task (Adapted from Open Up Resources):

Plot the points A (7,2), B (14,6), C (10,13), and D (3,9).

  a. Is ABCD a square? Explain how you know.

  b. Find the perimeter and area of the quadrilateral.

Refined Task:

Every few years, the neighborhood clean-up crew goes through the Hollow neighborhood to assist their elderly neighbors with major and minor home renovations. This year we will assist 7 neighbors to paint the fences outside their homes, and 1 neighbor will get a full exterior painting job. In estimating the amount of paint needed for the exterior job, we were given the coordinates of the house in feet (0, 0), (16, 0), (0, 24), and (16, 24). To determine the amount of paint, we need to multiply the perimeter of the home by the height. The height of the home is 18 feet.

  a. If we estimate that we can cover 350 square feet per gallon of paint, how much paint will we need? How much is the cost of the paint? Check the current price of 5 gallons of exterior paint.

  b. We will need about $\frac{3}{4}$ of a gallon of paint for each fence. How much paint will we need to paint all the fences?

  c. How might this project be adjusted to make a difference in a community you are familiar with?

IMPROVE

Think about a current community issue or project that interests you and/or your students. Search your mathematics curriculum for a task that can be adapted to address this issue. How can you stand in solidarity with the community?

Neighborhood beautification represents issues that come with community buy-in and often originate in common aims where people have already come together to formalize a plan. Reframing a task as we did centers the agency of standing in solidarity with the community cause. Additionally, there is a clear underlying message of supporting senior residents and their value to the community. The tradition of respecting and taking care of the elders in our communities is highlighted, and students can be encouraged to provide more details for the class based on their personal connections.

CREATING PROMPTS FROM MEDIA AND CURRENT ISSUES

Critical literacy is an important aim in English language arts standards, and it can—and should—also be applied to mathematics instruction. Consider the following excerpt from the National Council of Teachers of English (2020) website, NCTE.org:

> Critical literacy should be viewed as a lens, frame, or perspective for teaching throughout the day, across the curriculum, and perhaps beyond, rather than as a topic to be covered or unit to be studied. What this means is that critical literacy involves having an ingrained critical perspective or way of being that provides us with an ongoing critical orientation to texts and practices. Inviting students to write down the messages that they see in public transport, to take photographs of graffiti or billboards, to cut out advertisements from magazines, or to collect sweet wrappers to bring to class helps them to read the everyday texts they encounter critically. Do it often enough and they will learn to "read" their worlds with a critical eye.

Notice that the NCTE extends this notion of critical reading beyond books (although books are great places to begin) to an examination of the many messages our young people see in public. For the purposes of this discussion, we will ask that you extend this as well to all the different types of media outlets, including social media, advertising, music, television platforms, and movies.

Adolescence is a period when students spend a lot of time exploring their identity and learning independence. Popular culture plays a large role in this process in middle and high school. For many adolescents, pop culture includes comic books, video games, movies, television, and music, not to mention the more insidious (and not always positive) messaging they get through advertising and social media.

A great example of a pop culture phenomenon that can be harnessed by teachers to promote a positive identity for Black students is the Marvel character Black Panther. Not only was the 2018 movie a huge blockbuster, but the character has made numerous appearances in various television shows, animated films, video games, music, and the original comic book. The story explores a myriad of important issues, including Black imagination, identity, colonialism, and fighting for what's right. Teachers can structure empowering (and engaging) math lessons set in the fictional world of Wakanda. For example, students might consider quantities and problems associated

IMAGINE

Think about a teen media resource that has an important message or experience around agency. Now, think about how you can use that principle of agency in a mathematics task.

IMAGINE

After viewing the movie *Black Panther*, create a list of possible mathematical ideas to explore with high school students. Cooperative economics might be one idea. For example, students might be familiar with pop-up markets for small business owners in the community. How might you help connect these ideas with broader cultural or social themes relevant in the real world?

with the mining and market of the fictional "vibranium" as a resource, while simultaneously wondering if the vibranium should be shared with the world.

ASK

Reflect on the social issues that affect the community of the students you serve. What are some lesson topics that could support solidarity and belonging?

Another way to build students' agency is to have them read nonfiction literature or articles. They can learn about the lives and accomplishments of historical figures from their culture, as well as learning about what people—including kids their own age—are doing currently to help their communities and the world. By learning about the struggles that people experience and then how they persevered and realized their dreams, students can begin to recognize their own resilience. Remember, this is ongoing work, and every attempt at building students' agency is a step in the right direction.

In addition to using popular media as a source of math prompts, current social issues are ripe with possibility for culturally relevant teaching. Think back to Figure 5.2 Approaching Cultural Inquiry From a "We" Perspective. When you consider the approach of We Notice, tasks can be constructed via prompts to explore how students sense and see issues they care about and how those issues show up in their lives and in their community. Likewise, it is essential that the community of teachers, students, and others reflect on where they stand with regard to issues of social/racial injustice. During these initial stages of inquiry, they can discuss and collaborate on individual and collective viewpoints on issues impacting the community. We Notice means teachers and students explore issues in depth both holistically and through mathematics structures and concepts. Both students and educators are challenged to wonder and think about these issues, to develop their own positions and ideas, and to respond with action. Consider the following inquiry activity:

Internet Tower Task

Imagine your state plans to use COVID-19 emergency education funding to install internet towers all over the state so that more families can have access to the internet. Starting with your school district, identify whether neighborhoods nearby might benefit from the proposed plans. As you state your case, consider the following:

a. What neighborhoods are within range of internet towers? Explain how you know and provide information on the distance we are from the nearest tower.

b.   Are added towers justified? Explain.

c.   In its first round of funding, let's propose that your state received $71 million to assist districts in improving internet coverage during the pandemic. Based on the proximity-to-tower data, create a plan and allocate the funding in the fairest way possible. Consider the impact on as many people as possible. Display the allocation with a graph and justify your plan and its impact.

d.   What are other ways legislators might improve internet connectivity for families?

The purpose of the Internet Tower task is to demonstrate how activities might draw from current and emerging issues—in this instance, the COVID-19 pandemic and internet connectivity. During the COVID-19 pandemic, some students had a difficult time finding reliable internet service. There were a variety of reasons for this, including what has been commonly termed "the digital divide" (i.e., not having a computer or internet service at home; not living within range of an internet tower; having too many users in a household, hence, slowing down service; etc.). Some schools were able to accommodate the divide by providing spaces near schools as internet hotspots, using buses with internet, and providing students with take-home devices. In order to engage students themselves in tackling some of the issues of connectivity, they are prompted to explore the depth of the problem and the feasibility of a potential solution.

Adolescents understand the ramifications of living in a pandemic on a personal level and know the impact that the internet has had on their lives, but this question asks students to think beyond themselves to imagine what it might be like to live in a neighborhood where the internet is not available. Even teenagers are able to see that unfairness and disparity exist all around them. Learning to respond with empathy—and with mathematics—helps them grow as both compassionate community members and math doers.

Notice in the last prompt that we closed the task by asking students to consider how to help (take action). There are a great many opportunities to learn from the short context given here. For example, this task may lead to some discussion around the "why" of internet access and for "whom" it exists. Although we acknowledge that there is great care needed for such conversations, the teacher's role here is to adapt and create tasks for this possibility.

ASK

How do you know when to push exploration into difficult topics? What is key to handling such interactions with care and empathy?

Now, consider the following high school standard and task:

Shingle Mountain Task

Common Core State Standard: CCSS MATH CONTENT HSG.GMD.A.3

Use volume formulas for cylinders, pyramids, cones, and spheres to solve problems.

Task:

Most rooftops are covered by shingles, which take approximately 300 years to decompose in a landfill. When a contractor replaces a roof, the shingles should be disposed of in a safe way. A recycling company purchased land in an urban city for contractors to dump their shingles so the company could grind them to be repurposed for building roads. Unfortunately, the shingles were only dumped and not recycled, forming a mound that grew so large it became known in the community as "Shingle Mountain." In addition to this being an eyesore, it was next to a neighborhood and caused health issues for the residents. Several years after a resident filed a complaint with the city, the recycling company was ordered to remove the mountain (Fears, 2020). The trucks used to haul the shingles had beds shaped like a cylinder that was cut in half.

   a. If a dump truck is 8.5 feet wide and 36 feet long and 1 ton = 40 cu. ft., about how many tons can each truck haul?

   b. Shingle Mountain had a total of 154,396.2 tons. On the most productive day of removal, 5,491.81 tons were removed. If they kept up at that rate (5,491.81 tons removed per day), about how many truckloads were used to remove the entire mountain?

   c. If they used a truck with a bed shaped like a rectangular prism with the same dimensions, how many days would it have taken to remove the entire mountain?

   d. The project took a total of 9,098 trips over 70 nonconsecutive days. About how many trips (truckloads) were removed per day?

   e. Is there an environmental issue in your community similar to "Shingle Mountain"? What are some ways you might take action to help?

Students often hear about the importance of recycling, and many are active in helping preserve our environment, making it a familiar topic. This task is an example of recycling gone bad and who it affects. The shingles were dumped in a part of town that was zoned for industrial manufacturing even though it is very close to a residential area, so this task can lead to discussions about zoning, districting, and the importance of residents speaking out about the advantages and disadvantages of zoning and who can be adversely affected in many circumstances.

Summary and Discussion Questions

In this chapter, we offered three approaches for mathematical task building to nurture agency and action: selecting topics for critical contexts and action through social justice standards; building empathy; promoting agency and action through personal and collective empowerment; and creating prompts from media and current social issues. We shared some strategies for selecting topics for tasks, using the example of the Southern Poverty Law Center's *Learning for Justice* website as a great place to start with their social justice standards. The topics can be applied to the contexts of individual and personal empowerment, supporting community aspirations, and in solidarity with emerging social and racial justice issues. Before moving on to the next chapter where we explore notions of culturally relevant teaching and look at how teachers improve and implement culturally relevant tasks, consider the following questions:

1. Our first approach to task building is selecting topics for critical contexts and action through social justice standards. Using your district curriculum as a starting place and the social justice standards as a guide, focus on one existing task to begin to modify the context into one that is culturally relevant.
2. When you select or create a task with the goal of individual or collective empowerment for your students, what are some components or aspects that are essential to the task and the experience for your students?
3. Some students watch the news with their parents and engage in age-appropriate conversations about current events, such as the pandemic and racial justice. In what ways do you make emerging social and racial justice issues age-appropriate to incorporate math tasks with your students?

PART III

Refining Our Notions and Experiences

In Part III, we will share about our work with established and early career teachers and teacher leaders in their journey to understand culturally relevant mathematics teaching (CRMT) and interpret and implement Culturally Relevant Math Tasks into lessons and units. We will also share how culturally relevant tasks fit in a common teaching approach called teaching through problem-solving, along with other selected tools that have been created and refined by teachers.

CHAPTER 7

The Journey: Improving Culturally Relevant Mathematics Teaching

In this chapter, we will

1. Explore teachers' and leaders' emerging notions of culturally relevant teaching
2. Discuss how teachers can push beyond surface notions of culture
3. Advocate how teachers can better attend to agency
4. Explore how to improve culturally relevant mathematics teaching through an antiracist lens

In the last three chapters, we introduced and explored 12 approaches for creating and adapting CRMTasks, and you have taken an important step in learning some design approaches. Remember the foundation we laid in Chapter 1—culturally relevant mathematics tasks prioritize and challenge students as doers and creators of mathematics; position culture and community as central drivers of math inquiry; and target agency, empathy, and action. Such tasks make culturally relevant teaching possible and are meant to serve as anchors for inspiring lessons. But designing CRMTasks should not be seen as a magic pill. Task building is just one critical competence in the journey of teachers and leaders to create worthwhile mathematics engagement and opportunity. In this chapter, we aim to help you along this journey by revisiting our experiences with teachers and leaders on similar journeys.

IMPROVING TEACHERS' AND LEADERS' EMERGING NOTIONS OF CULTURALLY RELEVANT TEACHING

It's important to acknowledge that sustaining culturally relevant teaching in mathematics is a careerlong journey where teachers and leaders challenge, reject, disrupt, and grow their own notions of how math can be experienced, what the experience should look like, and what purposes it serves. Our experiences have taught us that what teachers believe and understand directly determines how successful they are in creating and teaching culturally relevant mathematics tasks. We consider this under-standing *emerging* in similar ways as we have viewed the task rubric earlier in the book. In this chapter, we share and examine how teachers and educational leaders interpret notions of cultur-ally relevant mathematics teaching and apply them for practice. We'll also analyze their work in the context of CRMTask-building as well as teaching, which we hope will encourage you to reflect on these issues in your own teaching (see Figure 7.1).

Sustaining culturally relevant teaching in mathematics is a careerlong journey where teachers and leaders challenge, reject, disrupt, and grow their own notions of how math can be experienced, what the experience should look like, and what purposes it serves.

FIGURE 7.1 ● Culturally relevant mathematics task-building actions

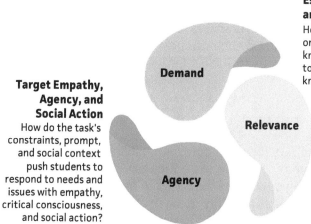

Establish Demand and Access

How does the task focus on building deep conceptual knowledge and prompt children to do and create mathematical knowledge?

Target Empathy, Agency, and Social Action

How do the task's constraints, prompt, and social context push students to respond to needs and issues with empathy, critical consciousness, and social action?

Center Community and Cultural Inquiry

How is the context and mathematical inquiry rooted in affirming and exploring cultural knowledges and identities? Does the task context and prompt feature empowered relationships, understandings about their community and themselves?

Demand

Relevance

Agency

CULTURALLY RELEVANT TEACHING AS MAKING MEANINGFUL CONNECTIONS

Exploring the perspectives of early career teachers is a good place to start in our discussion of *the journey*. In an undergraduate Math and Diverse Cultures course, Shelly once asked new teachers to write their personal definitions of culturally relevant teaching. Teachers were asked to respond without looking up any information so their thoughts could be authentic. There were several themes that emerged from their definitions, which align with much of what we have discussed previously in this book. One consistent acknowledgment was that they need to "make meaningful connections to students in order to help students feel important and engaged, which will in turn help them do better on their assignments." Many wrote about how they need to "tailor the work based on students' day-to-day lives, their learning styles, and their interests."

IMPROVE

Go deeper. For *what* purpose, and *for whom*, do we make mathematics meaningful?

Even though they are new to the field, these teachers already understand that making connections to students' real lives is an effective instructional strategy and that academic success is part of the goal. These new teachers were also aware that culturally relevant teaching requires the teacher to learn about different cultures within their classroom. What is missing from their current knowledge is the need to center their instruction in cultural and community inquiry (Relevance). This means going beyond merely inserting tidbits of information about students' interests, cultures, and learning styles. The idea is for the new teachers to learn how to create opportunities that empower students by engaging them in mathematics inquiry that affirms their culture and community. The component of *agency* was missing from these teachers' understanding as well. They have not yet understood the potential for their work to require students to critically examine issues leading to social action.

CULTURALLY RELEVANT TEACHING AS WORKING WITH CULTURE ONLY

Even when teachers focus on culture, it isn't enough to sustain culturally relevant teaching. As educators participate in professional learning opportunities directed at learning about culturally relevant teaching, they grow in their knowledge about what it entails. In one such professional development setting, we asked a group of teachers to write three words or short phrases to describe culturally relevant teaching. Again, we were not surprised. Many of the teachers responded with the words "relevant," "culture," and "equity." Other common responses focused on knowing who your students are in their day-to-day lives, their socioeconomic status, their language, and about students' communities. These experienced teachers had more knowledge about individual students and the local community because (1) they were current classroom teachers and thus had experiences to pull from and (2) their school district was participating in a districtwide "Diversity and Inclusiveness" initiative. The teachers also acknowledged that in order to teach from a culturally relevant perspective they needed to be flexible in their planning, as well as sensitive to and respectful of students' differences. One teacher made the point that students' life experiences are different and that doesn't mean the experiences should be looked at as limited. Although the teachers agreed with these notions of culturally relevant teaching, they acknowledged that this type of planning and teaching was not currently happening, and major changes in the way they plan and teach mathematics would be required.

Personal notions of culturally relevant teaching are not sufficient drivers for powerful mathematics experiences.

Personal notions of culturally relevant teaching are not sufficient drivers for powerful mathematics experiences. Teachers and leaders need to probe deeply into the well-constructed literature around such terms as culturally relevant, culturally responsive, and culturally sustaining. In the next sections, we tackle this process of moving deeper.

MOVING BEYOND THE SURFACE: DEEPENING CULTURAL EXPLORATIONS WHILE DOING MATH

In the spring of 2020, Lou and Shelly were invited to work virtually with an undergraduate class of preservice teachers who had just finished a student teaching practicum in the early days of the COVID-19 pandemic. The teachers were in the midst of "stay-home" periods common during the pandemic. Our purpose for the minisession was to have teachers reflect, and at times confront, their imagery of student communities and culture head-on. Ultimately, we hoped that the teachers might pledge to dig deeper to understand the ethnic culture/community around them. As you see in the sequence of slides in Figure 7.2, we first asked teachers to pause and consider what they learned about their own families during the pandemic (Slide 1).

As we expected, one outcome of the pandemic stay-home order was that families had to spend extra time together. Many of the teachers recounted words and phrases like "resilience" or "my family is really funny" or "stronger than I imagined." We asked them to also make a list of the same for their students (Slide 2). They were then asked to compare both sets of descriptions using Zaretta Hammond's (2014) *culture tree*, which describes tiers of cultural knowledge from observable surface level (food, music) to deeper level understandings of worldviews and core beliefs (Slide 3).

The anticipated dissonance in the ways in which teachers described their families versus their students was stark. In general, the descriptions of teachers' own family members were rich, inspiring, empathic, and empowering. The descriptions of students, on the other hand, were generally surface-level. We used this dissonance as a way to enter into group discussion (Slide 4) about the ways that mathematics might draw from cultural strengths and aspirations.

IMAGINE

Consider the activity using the culture tree. Share one powerful and inspiring feature of your family or friend group that you have witnessed lately. Reflect on the "story" of this revelation. What powerful and inspirational things do you know about your students and their families?

We see activities where teachers come into direct interrogation of their orientation and assumptions as critical to task building. Culturally relevant mathematics teaching requires an empowerment orientation where students' identity and home culture is further affirmed through mathematical activity. In reality, teachers can't learn about student culture without a simultaneous and continuous rejection of the harmful deficit narratives about those same cultures and the privileged position of dominant culture. A further extension of this focus on deeper understanding (remember Figure 2.3 Expand Understandings in the Culturally Relevant Mathematics Practices) is to apply these probing questions to how teachers select tasks, assignments, readings, and contexts to build Relevance with students.

When teachers start learning about students' cultures, it can be uncomfortable at times because teachers don't want to perpetuate stereotypes. This is a legitimate concern, which we will explore in the next section about confronting "difference" in culturally relevant teaching. Unfortunately, this fear often causes teachers to still choose to teach from a "color-blind" orientation. They think that by not "seeing" race or culture they can treat everyone the same. However, this thinking does quite the opposite. Students receive the message that their whole selves are not welcome in the classroom. It renders students of color invisible and causes them to try to leave their culture at home, which is impossible to do.

FIGURE 7.2 ● Selected presentation slides from an undergraduate preservice teacher seminar at Illinois State University on April 29, 2020

In the Chat Window	Break-Out Groups
Share one powerful, inspiring strength you realized about you and your family during the Covid-19 "stay-home" period	Make a group list of powerful, inspiring strengths you realized about your students and their families during the Covid-19 "stay-home" period

Levels of Culture

- **Observable elements:** food, music, dress, holidays low emotional charge
- **Unspoken rules, social norms:** nonverbal communication, eye contact, personal space strong emotional charge
- **Worldview,** core beliefs, group values
- **Cultural archetypes** such as collective vs. individual
- **Mental models,** funds of knowledge INTENSE emotional charge

Surface
Shallow
Deep

"What's Culture Got to Do With It?" *Culturally Responsive Teaching and the Brain: Promoting Authentic Engagement and Rigor among Culturally and Linguistically Diverse Students,* by Zaretta Hammond and Yvette Jackson, Corwin, a SAGE Company, 2015. ●

Group Discussion

- How should learning and teaching about mathematics be shifted or remixed in ways that draw from cultural strengths and aspirations?
- What are examples from the cultural tree (assets) that drive the decisions you would make? Where is the information you know?

Questions to Consider

We know (even from our sample of 22 student teachers) that schools in IL are approaching remote learning in a variety of ways.

- What do you know about the variation in approaches across schools?
- What factors are influencing this variation? How does this connect to what you know about your students and their communities?
- How can you make the most of this time (now)?

More Questions

We know (even from our sample of 22 student teachers) that schools in IL are approaching remote learning in a variety of ways.

- What are and will be the effects of this variation?
- What is your role as mathematics teachers in supporting students, especially in the context of these overt inequities?
- What do we do in the fall? How can you build on student assets?

Needing to go deeper with cultural inquiry will be part of the journey for all mathematics educators. Let's revisit the teacher in Chapter 2 with their summer STEM students, where an icebreaker activity garnered the teacher a new understanding of their students. The activity asked students to write three hashtags that would describe them as a person. One student wrote #Muslim, and another student chimed in, "I'm Muslim too." In a later activity, Maryam, the student who wrote the #Muslim hashtag, brought in a photograph of a sofa in her home that had an Islamic tessellation pattern. This prompted the teacher to do a follow-up lesson on Islamic tessellations. Although this experience of making connections to students' culture was new for the teacher, they knew they could not stop at the tessellation activity.

The teacher decided to do some research on resources they might use in the classroom to inspire (Hope verb) students from the Islamic culture. In addition to the lesson highlighting the beauty and mathematical importance of Islamic tessellations, the first idea that came to mind was to highlight the life and work of Maryam Mirzakhani, an Iranian American mathematician. The teacher was excited about the prospect of broadening the representation of who these students see as mathematicians.

Maryam Mirzakhani was born in Iran and followed the Islamic religion. She was the first, and at this time, the only woman to be awarded the prestigious Fields Medal. She earned a doctorate degree from Harvard University and was a professor at Stanford University. While a teenager, Maryam became interested in mathematics when her brother showed her a math problem he was doing in school. The problem was to add the numbers from 1 to 100. Maryam once said, "The more I spend time on maths, the more excited I get." She called herself a "slow" mathematician. Dr. Mirzakhani was known as a theoretical mathematician. Although most of the mathematics she worked on did not have an immediate real-world application, it did have implications for the study of prime numbers and cryptography. When Dr. Mirzakhani passed away in 2017, she was remembered all over the world. In particular, some of the newspapers in her home country of Iran broke with the country's strict rules on female dress by featuring Dr. Mirzakhani without a hijab. They wanted to remember her as she lived.

ASK

How does the example about Maryam Mirzakhani represent an empowerment orientation toward student identity and culture?

By taking the time to search for a resource to connect to the identity of this one student, the teacher is able to affirm how this student belongs in math.

Culturally relevant mathematics teaching requires an empowerment orientation where students' identity and home culture is further affirmed through mathematical activity.

CONFRONTING "DIFFERENCE" IN CULTURALLY RELEVANT TEACHING

One of the challenges we see with teachers' definitions of culturally relevant teaching is the focus on the word "different"— different cultures, different languages, different traditions, different backgrounds, and differences between students. The portrayal of differences in this way can be seen as "othering." Othering describes the ways in which people and groups are portrayed as different, and the differences are translated as inferior to the dominant culture. For example, when we refer to students as English language learners, it is often pointed out what students *don't* know—they are learning the English language—as opposed to positioning them from an asset-based perspective—multilingual learners—because they *do* have language *and* they are learning multiple languages.

ASK

How is language framed and used in mathematics experiences for students in your current school environment? In what ways are "differences" acknowledged or framed?

Why is it so important to value and affirm differences like cultural language when practicing CRMT? One teacher wrote about the idea of difference in this way, saying that culturally relevant teaching is about "respecting the diversity of the students and using their unique differences to create an educational environment that is welcoming and respectful." Another teacher wrote about finding out what students have in common and using that in a lesson. A third teacher talked about connecting lessons to the past so that students can learn about the diverse cultures that contributed to the development of mathematics. When we learn about our students in their own voices, we can begin to see the value in their stories. You will be able to move beyond stereotypes, especially those that are derogatory.

When we learn about our students in their own voices, we can begin to see the value in their stories.

Another important idea arising from our conversations with teachers was for students to learn about cultures from around the world in order to have a "window" view. We believe students must have opportunities to see themselves in the curriculum (mirror view) as well as opportunities to be exposed to the broader world (window view). A mirror view would involve the teacher using students' interests, community funds of knowledge, and the like to have the mathematics reflect something the student has prior knowledge about and something that honors students, their families, and their communities. A window view could provide opportunities for students to learn about different family traditions—for example, some families have a tradition of making and flying kites, while other families have a special game night, and others look forward to an annual camping trip. All of these activities are windows for students who are unfamiliar with them. For a more global view, a teacher could introduce students to different number systems and currency from countries other than the United States. This can be challenging for teachers to implement because often school

ASK

How will you build your capacity to think more deeply about local and global situations that impact your students' daily lives and their futures?

districts have set math curricula that teachers must follow. But we contend that even with a set curriculum, teachers can find opportunities to make choices about the contexts for teaching a given math content area.

IMPROVING UNDERSTANDINGS OF CULTURE AS A SOURCE FOR BUILDING AGENCY

CRMT offers an alternative approach to teaching mathematics that capitalizes on students' rich cultural backgrounds. Both students and teachers become more culturally competent when using CRMTasks. When teachers are culturally competent, they are able to move beyond, for instance, simply using ethnically diverse names in word problems. They will develop relationships with their students such that cultural references become a natural part of planning mathematics lessons.

What happens when teachers work toward agency while teaching? In her work with teachers, Shelly found that several themes emerged when teachers attempted to plan lessons using an agency lens. Teachers planned lessons that (1) empowered students to make changes in their lives, (2) helped students become more aware of issues that affect them, and (3) attended to students' identities. However, teachers continued to struggle to plan math lessons that had a critical component. In essence, teaching math for social justice eluded these teachers (Jones, 2018).

To assist teachers with building students' agency, we suggest that they become a part of the community of the students they serve. They can do this by establishing trusting relationships with parents, guardians, and community members at after-school activities and community events. Building relationships in and out of the academic space is important in order to establish a deeper understanding of students' multiple identities and the community culture, as well as to expose the benefits of such an understanding. Teachers should collaborate with parents and community members as intellectual partners by inviting them to participate in lessons as experts in math content areas relevant to their careers or community work (Civil & Andrade, 2003).

As teachers connect with students and the community, they have greater opportunities to learn about the issues that are important to that community. These issues will provide the basis for teachers to plan lessons that empower students through agency and social action. Teachers gain more confidence to teach math for social justice when they understand their students and the local context. Although it is customary for students to learn from their teachers, teachers can—and should—learn from their students as well. Students feel safe in their classroom when they feel that the teacher understands them and appreciates who they are. One teacher said it this way:

> *Culturally relevant teaching is recognizing the importance of including students' backgrounds or lived experiences in all aspects of teaching and learning within the classroom and across the school environment. [Teachers must] acknowledge where all [their] students come from and what they go through or experience on a day-to-day basis. Knowing where your students come from can be very encouraging for your students and could make them less scared to participate or less scared of feeling judged. It can empower them intellectually, emotionally, and politically.*

IMPROVE

What are some questions/thoughts your students have about a current issue in your school or community? Using mathematics, how can students explore and confront this issue?

We talked about the importance of students seeing themselves in mathematics lessons and how teachers can create lessons by getting to know their students and their communities. It is also important that students are exposed to representation of mathematicians who look like them. When we asked teachers to think about a mathematician, who do you think came to mind? Most educators named Einstein, Fermat, Euler, or Pythagoras. On the other hand, we also have the 2017 *Hidden Figures* film to thank for Katherine Johnson, Dorothy Vaughan, Mary Jackson, and Christine Darden that educators have learned about lately and are now able to feature in mathematics lessons.

If you'd like a more diverse representation of mathematicians to share with your students, we provided a short list of websites in Chapter 2, including *Mathematically Gifted & Black* (www.mathematicallygiftedandblack.com), *Lathisms* (www.lathisms.org), and *Indigenous Mathematicians* (www.indigenousmethematicians.org). Another great resource for exposing students to contemporary mathematicians from diverse backgrounds is the *Meet a Mathematician* video interview series at www.meetamathematician.com. These resources can be used to highlight the work of diverse mathematicians, which can motivate students who don't see themselves in traditional mathematics curriculum spaces. In addition to website resources, you may also use literature as a way to make cultural connections to mathematics (see Chapter 5). For teaching mathematics for social justice, we provided ideas from the *Learning for Justice* website in Chapter 6.

SEEING CULTURALLY RELEVANT TEACHING AS ANTIRACIST

During a professional learning (PL) session with mathematics education leaders, Shelly posed the same question she asked the teachers mentioned earlier in the chapter—to brainstorm three words or short phrases to describe culturally relevant teaching/pedagogy. This leadership team had recently participated in a book study on how to become antiracist educators. The most popular words leaders offered to describe CRP were "equitable," "inclusive," and "antiracist." Other words mentioned by multiple leaders were "relationships," "empower," "student-centered," "identity," and "unbiased." The descriptors from all three groups of educators—new teachers, experienced teachers, and teacher leaders—are listed in Figure 7.3 and loosely fit into one of three themes: Relevance, Equity, and Inclusiveness.

FIGURE 7.3 ● Themes in educators' notions of culturally relevant pedagogy

MAKING MATHEMATICS RELEVANT	CREATING EQUITABLE MATHEMATICS	CREATING INCLUSIVE SPACES
Community	Accessible, access for all	Accepting
Connections	Differentiated	Awareness
Engaging	Economics	Diverse
Global	Informal	Embrace
Important	Multifaceted	Empathy
Interests	Multiple entry points	Encouraging
Linguistic	Open	Flexible
Local	Rigorous	Identity
Relatable	Student-centered	Mindset
Relevant	Vocabulary	Moral
		Relationships
		Respect
		Sensitive
		Unbiased

ASK

How do the themes identified by educators compare to the dimensions of the CRCD mathematics task rubric (Figure 3.3)? Where would tasks based on these themes fall on the spectrum of Emerging, Developing, and Exemplary?

Of the three groups we worked with, the leaders' descriptions of culturally relevant teaching were most aligned with our notion of Agency. These leaders expressed an understanding that culturally relevant experiences require that students use critical mathematical thinking to challenge the inequities that exist in our society so that they will be able to make empowered decisions about themselves and their communities. Of the three groups, the leaders were the only group who participated in a PL opportunity that introduced them to the notion of antiracism in education. Their discussions during the sessions focused on how to orchestrate opportunities for teachers to rehumanize mathematics instruction through equitable, inclusive, and antiracist instruction and curriculum. The leader group was the only group that described culturally relevant teaching in these more active terms. They recognized that school structures produce racialized outcomes. The fact that this was seen with the leaders may be because the kind of training necessary to address agency may not be seen as critical at the practitioner level. We believe it is. The targeting of agency invokes the critical component of culturally relevant teaching. Teachers and students who acquire a critical consciousness build agency for racial justice. This requires intentional—and careful—planning learning opportunities where teachers and leaders participate in uncomfortable conversations about who is privileged in our current mathematics education system.

Summary and Discussion Questions

In this chapter, we discussed some ways in which teachers and leaders view culturally relevant teaching. We explored these views using the definition of culturally relevant mathematics teaching we have been drawing from in this book. Practitioners often invoke varied, perhaps less robust, definitions of culturally relevant teaching. Many are challenged to think of culture in ways that do not "other" the students, but affirm and empower students in a welcoming and respectful way. As you use culturally relevant mathematics tasks to create lessons and units for culturally relevant teaching, you may find yourself addressing these varied notions. Consider the following as you think through the improvement process and implement tasks to incorporate into culturally relevant experiences:

1. As you reflect on what you learned early in your practice, how have your ideas about culturally relevant teaching shifted? How have you revised your idea of culturally relevant teaching? What thoughts and ideas you already had have been further confirmed?

2. Choose a mathematics task or lesson that you are already using in your classroom or have used in the past. In what ways did students respond? How did their responses point back to your application of culturally relevant teaching? What would you change? What went well that you will keep and develop further?

3. In the examples in the chapter, we see the differences in understanding among teachers, teacher leaders, and leaders. Do you believe a movement of change is possible in your school or organization environment? What professional learning opportunities would be needed to build robust understanding of culturally relevant teaching?

CHAPTER 8

The Flow: Implementing and Refining Culturally Relevant Tasks, Lessons, and Units

In this chapter, we will

1. Revise tasks to be more culturally relevant using a template

2. Adapt and explore the three-part lesson for implementing culturally relevant mathematics teaching and tasks

3. Examine the flow of a curriculum unit composed of teacher-created culturally relevant mathematics tasks

Now that you've gained an understanding of what culturally relevant mathematics teaching is and what culturally relevant mathematics tasks are, let's continue to explore how CRMTasks and teaching can be implemented in lessons and units that aim to promote engagement and challenge. We will start by navigating a process for refining mathematics tasks using a template, then broaden our scope by exploring a lesson approach called *Teaching Through Problem Solving* (Van de Walle, 2013), or the three-part lesson structure, also referred to in phases of "Before, During, and After" or "Launch, Explore, and Congress." Teaching through problem-solving is a particularly robust approach that has great potential for illuminating the possibilities for culturally relevant teaching. For purposes of this chapter, we will use the terminology of Launch–Explore–Culminate/Congress as we describe how to adapt the three-part lesson to teaching culturally relevant mathematics. Building on what we've learned about culturally relevant teaching on the task and lesson level, we will then examine the flow of a teacher-made curriculum unit.

WORKING WITH A MATH TASK TEMPLATE

To assist teachers in the process of creating CRMTasks, we developed a template for revising a task to be culturally relevant. It is a tool for thinking through the process of task revision as well as training for future task creation work.

Using the template in Figure 8.1, teachers can choose and evaluate a current task from their curriculum in order to increase the level of cultural relevance of the task from its current state (in Chapter 3, we provided suggestions under task-building actions on how to select a math task that lends itself to revision for cultural relevance). The template then reminds teachers of several strategies for getting started in the revision process. The first question teachers should consider when embarking on this work is, What about the task am I trying to revise, and how will I revise it? After revising the task, teachers should ask themselves how the task empowers students. If they are unable to answer this question, then they must dig a little deeper to consider a different revision.

In the scenario in Figure 8.1, you can see how one in-service teacher used the Revising a Math Task to Be Culturally Relevant template to assist them in selecting a task from their curriculum and revising it to be culturally relevant. The teacher was reminded to refer to the CRCD math task rubric (Figure 3.3) while using the template (see Appendix A for a blank Revising a Math Task to Be Culturally Relevant template).

FIGURE 8.1 ● Completed Revising a Math Task to Be Culturally Relevant template

---

Octagonal Tessellation in Islamic Architecture

Goal: Describe the desired movement on the CRCD math task rubric (Emerging to Developing to Exemplary).

I wanted to move the original task, "Octagonal Tessellation in Islamic Architecture," from Emerging to Developing/close to Exemplary. The original task(s) was cognitively demanding but was "culturally neutral." By incorporating a "mirror" for a student in the class and "windows" for others, it became a culturally relevant task.

Original Task (Should be a cognitively demanding task)

The original tasks were a hexagon perimeter task and a pattern tile task.

Task 1. Each figure in the pattern below is made of hexagons that measure 1 centimeter on each side. If the pattern of adding one hexagon to each figure is continued, what will be the perimeter of the 25th figure in the pattern? Marcy has to determine the perimeter of the 25th figure, but she does not want to draw all 25 figures. Explain or show how she could do this <u>and</u> give the answer that Marcy should get for the perimeter.

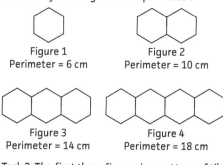

| Figure 1 | Figure 2 |
| Perimeter = 6 cm | Perimeter = 10 cm |

| Figure 3 | Figure 4 |
| Perimeter = 14 cm | Perimeter = 18 cm |

Task 2: The first three figures in a pattern of tiles are shown below. Describe the 20th figure in this pattern, including the total number of tiles it contains and how they are arranged. Then, explain the reasoning that you used to determine this information. Write a description that could be used to define any figure in the pattern. In other words, generalize the pattern. You may use words and/or an equation.

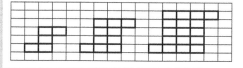

Math Content (Grade level State Standards)

CCSS.MATH.CONTENT.6.EE.A.2

Write, read, and evaluate expressions in which letters stand for numbers.

CCSS.MATH.CONTENT.6.EE.A.3

Apply the properties of operations to generate equivalent expressions. *For example, apply the distributive property to the expression 3 (2 + x) to produce the equivalent expression 6 + 3x; apply the distributive property to the expression 24x + 18y to produce the equivalent expression 6 (4x + 3y); apply properties of operations to y + y + y to produce the equivalent expression 3y.*

CCSS.MATH.CONTENT.6.EE.A.4

Identify when two expressions are equivalent (i.e., when the two expressions name the same number regardless of which value is substituted into them). *For example, the expressions y + y + y and 3y are equivalent because they name the same number regardless of which number y stands for.*

Why did you choose this task? What aspect of the task was the focus?

I used octagons instead of hexagons (because it fit the context better) and related it to Islamic architecture. I considered the "mirror/window" as I wanted to address a specific student in the class who is Muslim and was more withdrawn/not confident or participating in class much. I wanted to address her power/participation (Aguirre & Zavala, 2013) and math identity. For other students in the class, I wanted to create a "window" to learn about a different culture.

Using the CRCD math task rubric, describe how the math task was revised.

The original tasks had no context. Creating the context of tessellations in Islamic architecture addressed the "world around them" and cultural knowledge of Muslim/Islamic culture. Students also were able to connect this to their own lives/community by considering where there might be geometric patterns in their own community. I employed the Concrete-Representational-Abstract/Connections strategy throughout the lesson by first having students re-create the first three stages of a pattern using green and yellow octagons and extend it to the fourth stage (concrete), then students drew (colored) in the pattern on their paper and created a T-chart to show numerically how the pattern grew (representational). Next, students considered what the 20th stage would be and the "nth" stage using an expression (abstract). Finally, we compared how students saw the pattern and analyzed equivalent expressions (connections).

Revised CRMTask

Octagonal Tessellation in Islamic Architecture

 The octagonal designs in the Alhambra in Spain show various growth patterns in the tessellations. Each figure below demonstrates one such pattern that can be made with octagons. The first 3 figures represent sections of the complete tessellation. What would be the 4th figure (stage) of the pattern in this tessellation? What would the 20th figure be? Develop an explicit rule for any stage of the pattern in this tesselation.

How will this empower students?

It will empower students to learn more about their community by looking for geometric patterns in town. Also, as part of a closure/reflection in the lesson, the following question was proposed: How can we help our school learn more about the influences of Islamic culture on architecture in our community? This will help empower them by understanding the importance of learning about different cultural influences. It also empowers them because they are left to make the decision of how we could do this.

Figure 1   Figure 2   Figure 3

 To access a downloadable version of this figure, visit the *Engaging With Culturally Relevant Math Tasks (Secondary)* Free Resources tab on the Corwin website or visit https://bit.ly/3Lgv22E.

PLAN

Select a task from your current curriculum/textbook. Use the template to revise the task to be more culturally relevant. How did the template help you think through the planning process? Is there anything you would change/add to the template to make it more useful?

The teacher selected a cognitively demanding mathematics task and centered the new task in having students learning about locations in their community where they see geometry. They targeted agency and social action by having them (1) learn about their community, (2) learn about the Islamic culture, and (3) decide how they can share what is learned with the school community. This serves as a good example for beginning the process of implementing culturally relevant math tasks with students. Remember, the math task is the chief means for how students will participate and experience mathematics in the classroom. Therefore, it is important to continually consider how to revise your current tasks to be more culturally relevant. This template is another tool to assist you in that process. It will be helpful to also continue to refer to the CRMTask-Building Actions (Figure 7.1). For example, this task is centered on community and cultural inquiry.

As we have mentioned, tasks are foundational for the teaching and learning of mathematics. Therefore, starting with rigorous math tasks that are culturally relevant will serve as the basis for culturally relevant math lessons, units, and a cohesive culturally relevant mathematics curriculum. In the next section, we share an example of how a teacher began by revising a mathematics task and then used that task to revise an entire lesson to be more culturally relevant.

THE THREE-PART LESSON

The three-part lesson is predicated on the notion that students build powerful mathematical learning as they intentionally prepare to unlock mathematical thinking and experiences (*launch*). They can then actively explore their ideas and strategies (*explore*) and work with the teacher to build important understandings about their work and the work of others through dialogue, reflection, and extension (*culminate/congress*).

Launch
Teacher poses task and primes student prior knowledge and interest

Explore
Students use strategies and thinking to explore mathematics tasks

Culminate/Congress
Teacher and students build and refine new understandings of student strategies and thinking through discourse and extension

Each of these stages provides opportunities for thinking about how to use CRMTasks. Tasks are not created in isolation from the overall lesson design, so it is important to reflect deeply on the kind of lesson structure you will be dropping tasks into. Figure 8.2 shows how we expand the phases of three-part lesson planning to accommodate CRMTasks specifically and in general.

FIGURE 8.2 ● Adapted phases of three-part lesson for culturally relevant mathematics tasks

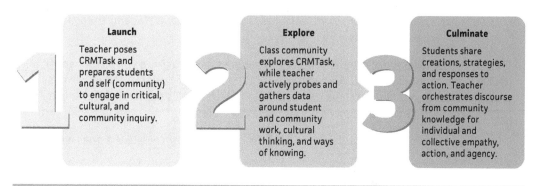

Launch
Teacher poses CRMTask and prepares students and self (community) to engage in critical, cultural, and community inquiry.

Explore
Class community explores CRMTask, while teacher actively probes and gathers data around student and community work, cultural thinking, and ways of knowing.

Culminate
Students share creations, strategies, and responses to action. Teacher orchestrates discourse from community knowledge for individual and collective empathy, action, and agency.

In Figure 8.3, we offer a culturally relevant teaching template to give you a view of how the three phases might show up as part of a lesson plan. Figure 8.4 features an example of a CRMT minilesson.

FIGURE 8.3 ● Culturally Relevant Teaching Lesson template

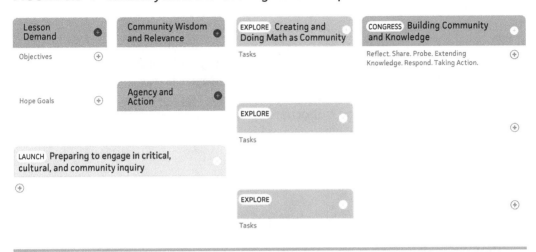

FIGURE 8.4 ● Sample CRMathematics minilesson

"Trying to Make a Dollar Outta Fifteen Cents"

Lesson Intention:

In this minilesson, participants delve into the issue of gentrification, food deserts, and urban sprawl by looking at the latest graphed expansion of two common neighborhood stores.

Math Standard: CCSS.MATH.CONTENT.HSF.IF.B.4 Interpret functions that arise in applications in terms of the context.

Launch:

Teacher poses culturally relevant, rich mathematics task and prepares students to engage in self, cultural, and community inquiry

Teacher poses questions: Where do you get your best bargains? Are you a Walmart or Dollar Store shopper? Do you live close to one? What kinds of discount stores are near your neighborhood? Do you think that this (your experience) is similar or different to urban neighborhoods in Baltimore or D.C.? Give examples.

Does the kind of neighborhood matter as to the location of stores like the ones we have mentioned?

Teacher poses: One of the important things we can do in mathematics is to look at relationships like store growth and location and make interpretations.

For this problem, I want you and your team to examine the graph below and use your knowledge of functions to make sense of issues like neighborhood grocery stores.

Grocery Sales at Dollar Stores and Whole Foods

Note: The figures for 'Dollar Stores' are the combined grocery sales of the dominant companies, Dollar General and Dollar Tree, which owns Family Dollar.
Source: Chain Store Guide

Identify the critical variables in the graph and describe how they are changing, if at all. What do you notice?

Using a cell phone or tablet, create a 2-minute video that "tells" the story of the graph (or create a presentation). In the video/presentation, address specifically how each situation changed for each store over the 7-year period and defend, justify, and challenge, if need be, the value of these stores for your community.

Explore

Students explore task. Teacher actively probes and gathers data on student and community work, cultural thinking, and ways of knowing. Students Engage in the activity in teams of 2 or 3. Pick a neighborhood or urban area that you and your team might be familiar with.

Culminate/Congress

Students share insights, strategies, and ways of knowing. Teacher orchestrates discussion, building individual and collective understanding, empowerment, and action. Teacher selects certain groups to share their video (or alternatively their presentation) to the class.

Teacher poses questions:

- How does your graph give you a visual representation of the story?

- How would changing an element (for example, adjusting the amount of sales at any given year) positively or negatively impact the story and alter the graph?

- What is the value of using a graphical representation in this and similar situations?

- How intense is the change? Can we consider slope as a key indicator here?

- What variables in the story are represented in the graph? How do these variables help you complete the story?

- How did you use the information to develop your story?

Action:

I want you to huddle with your groups and take on the role of an urban planner. How might you ally with communities who see this kind of expansion as a threat? How might this look compared to the graph above?

LAUNCH

In the launch phase of the three-part lesson, the teacher primes the learning by posing the task. For example, imagine a statistics lesson where the teacher plans to lead students to graph, represent, and interpret data that they've collected from a previous activity. To launch, the teacher simulates a sample of collected data among students—for example, after-school jobs or household chore responsibilities. Students call out their job while the teacher records their choices as tally marks. The ensuing discussion that takes place with students is to determine differences in where students work or what their household responsibilities are to help distinguish between similar but different choices, but also to determine what kind of graph might be needed to represent the data. Soon after, the students are turned loose at the end of the launch to explore and represent data that they have collected previously individually or in groups.

We see so much potential in the launch to enact culturally relevant mathematics teaching. Here, we ask teachers to actively consider not only posing a relevant entry into mathematics activity but also to give strong attention to engineering the conditions for intellectual, cultural, and critical inquiry. In the sections that follow, we stress the importance of prepping the internal and external environments.

LEAN IN TO THE SOCIAL/CULTURAL ENVIRONMENT

Every day, communities experience joy, thriving, and celebration along with the challenges of economics, health, and discrimination. Leaning in at the onset of the launch is key to centering and affirming the community/cultural space so that cultural and community inquiry can take place. What do we mean by leaning in? We see this as the act of becoming vulnerable for the purpose of empathizing and connecting with one's students and community. It's a hugely personal act, as illustrated by the example that follows:

LAUNCH

Ms. V takes some deep breaths as she sits on a stool in front of the class and shares a personal experience of growing up, playing in a neighborhood field that is now slated to become an upscale mall. She then prompts students to think about how their own neighborhoods have changed for them and their parents and to share their thoughts. After students share, they are then asked to calculate and compare the changing perimeters from a map of a local Washington, D.C., ward boundary from a decade earlier to the present time.

In the previous example, Ms. V leans in by centering a launch onto a personal experience that is very emotional for her. She then draws students into the experience as they reflect on their own neighborhoods. From the very beginning, the lesson is established as being personal and community-oriented.

MAKE SPACE

Too often, mathematics is practiced as an isolated experience inside the walls of the classroom. It is important to ask yourself how you can make room for the community around you and acknowledge the land or the people in it. Teachers who value community and culture take the community/cultural pulse of place and mind regularly (if not already immersed in it) and focus on this orientation from the onset of the learning experience. For example, a teacher might make a point to acknowledge the real impact of the nomination and confirmation of Justice Ketanji Brown Jackson to the United States Supreme Court for the Black communities and Black female students in the class:

> ### LAUNCH
>
> Ms. Collins draws from the moment to amplify representation of African American women in politics with a brief notice and wonder session. In the session, she shows her students a chart depicting the demographic representation of local elected offices and reiterates the notion that many Supreme Court Justices were once elected officials.

In the following example, the launch leans in to the public pulse around the Black Lives Matter movement and is designed to engage students:

> ### LAUNCH
>
> The teacher displays an aerial photo of a Black Lives Matter mural featured in a local news article. After probing student knowledge about the Black Lives Matter movement and the mural, the teacher prompts students to estimate how much space the mural takes up just by judging the photo. After fielding some estimates and reasoning from student estimates, the teacher asks students to propose phrases that might honor current social movements they care about.
>
>
>
> Source: https://www.courant.com/community/ bloomfield/hc-wn-bloomfield-public-art-0121– 20210115-cqzxzxxocvdyhnvyyz27gumn6i-story.html

"EVERYONE, TAKE A SEAT": SITUATE LEARNERS AS CO-CREATORS

A key component of the launch is the environment in which students are engaged in risk-taking, collaboration, and knowledge construction. By sharing power and space, teachers intentionally situate the learner at the table of math making. In launching tasks, teachers can provide opportunities for learners—and by extension the learner's community and cultures—by centering students as co-creators of both context and content.

LAUNCH

During Mrs. Han's algebra launch, a student tells of an experience starting a neighborhood business during the summer, after which the teacher solicits others to share experiences where they have sold a product or service. Eventually, the teacher poses a task where students set up functions and linear equations to solve word problems and representations involving business applications.

CREATE

What are some examples of instances where you can create launch spaces where students feel safe to use their voices and take risks? What are some things you can do to create a supportive environment for your students?

By creating space for students to share business experience, the teacher has created an environment that is primed for immediate community inquiry and discussion. This "student and community inquiry" is critical for understanding and centering culture in knowledge construction. In this way, teachers build on informal and cultural knowledge.

There is an important tension to illuminate here. You may feel inclined to make this space totally about students, in the sense that students create for and by themselves. We do not believe this is the true intent of culturally relevant pedagogy. CRP is centered on multiple interlocking communities that co-create together—the classroom, the family unit, the cultural community, the local community, and the global community. In this context, community itself can be defined as co-construction. In the classroom community, power is shared so that there are opportunities for students *and* teachers to create experiences and contexts that matter. The teacher's role is to guide this power sharing as both designer and facilitator. This is an opportunity to share—not surrender—the space so that students and their communities can engage in authentic inquiry.

In the classroom community, power is shared so that there are opportunities for students and teachers to create experiences and contexts that matter.

EXPLORE

In the exploration phase of three-part lessons, students have opportunities to *do* mathematics. When students explore, they use various strategies, communication, and tools to engage in the tasks. This part of the lesson phase is critical, and it's probably where the teacher learns the most about student understandings and misunderstandings. When students engage in this part of the lesson, they are *doing* mathematics because the teacher has chosen a task that requires enough cognitive effort such that students do not have an immediate solution strategy. Students may experience productive struggle during this phase because they are being asked to solve a problem that helps them to connect prior learning to new learning, not to merely follow a procedure.

The explore phase is also a great time during the lesson to have students work collaboratively. This way, as the teacher circulates throughout the classroom, they will have the opportunity to observe student written work and listen to student thinking through their conversations. We also see exploration as a time for listening and learning culturally. This is important for culturally relevant teaching because the teacher can continue to build on what they learned about students and community in the launch phase. It is important here to ask questions that build on and extend students' prior knowledge. By doing so, the teacher is helping to build student identity as doers and producers of math. When students are appropriately engaged during the explore phase, they begin to feel empowered, and this leads to building student agency.

Teachers are asked to record and collect data on what students do, how they think, and how they use strategies to solve challenging problems, such as in the following example.

EXPLORE

Ms. Etta introduced graphing linear equations by turning her classroom into a coordinate grid where each student was an (x,y) coordinate and pairs of students were connected by string to form various lines. The lesson took place after the football team had experienced an amazing victory in the final seconds due to an interception of the opposing team's final pass. The school's defensive player who made the interception, the cornerback, was a student in her class. When she brought up the y-intercept, she congratulated him on his impressive play and had him lead the students in standing in as coordinates to demonstrate the play.

This example shows the teacher noticing y-intercept and interceptions, but it also gives great insight into what cultural noticing looks like. A close inspection reveals that there is a connection to football, which the teacher recognizes and then allows the students to take the lead.

Let's revisit the Black Lives Matter (BLM) task. Remember during the launch phase, the teacher prepared students to engage in community inquiry. She asked about social movements they cared about. In the explore phase, the teacher poses the Google Maps task.

Use Google Maps to find the map of the BLM mural (aerial view) in Bloomfield, Connecticut, or find the map of a circular region in your community.

1. Use the measurement tool in Google Maps to measure the diameter, radius, and circumference of the exterior and interior circles of the circular region.

2. Determine the area of the circular region to be painted.

3. Determine the amount of paint you will need to cover the mural's background with a primer color.

4. Calculate the cost of the paint.

5. Determine the approximate amount of paint and cost for each section (each letter and spaces) of your mural phrase—for example, if you use the Black Lives Matter phrase you could divide the circle into 19 sections (to account for the letters, blank spaces, and the fist).

For teaching using culturally relevant mathematics tasks, we extend the notion of "noticing" and "recording" to ask teachers to think intentionally about the many ways in which cultural thinking is showing up. Note that *cultural* thinking is used here in place of the more commonly used *informal* thinking to emphasize the importance of deliberately attending to notions of cultural ways of knowing, affirmation, celebration, and solidarity. This speaks to the biggest challenge we see for aspiring teachers of CRMT in that teachers do not invest enough in what Ladson-Billings calls "mining" (1994). Teachers are often limited by lack of knowledge, lack of will, and bias. We challenge you here to consider questions like "Why is this problem strategy important to **us**?"—with emphasis on the "us." When engaging with students as they do math, you can ask yourself, In what ways are community ways of knowing affirmed, validated, or celebrated through the use of this particular response to the problem?

CULMINATE/CONGRESS

In the culmination part of the lesson, the teacher utilizes the collected data about student thinking, strategies, and understandings (and misunderstandings) acquired in the explore phase. This data is used to facilitate active discourse during which students can make sense of their ideas and refine them in new and more sophisticated ways. Using CRMTasks, we can extend this to create space for students to share co-creations, strategies, feelings, empathy, and responses to action. For example, extending the *explore* example on linear equations, the teacher might realize connections between other sports and linear equations and wish to find out more information in the culmination/congress phase. As a result, the teacher and class learn more about activities in which the students are engaging that are important to them and which might emphasize graphing. During the culminate phase of the Black Lives Matter task, the teacher discusses with students the phrases they chose and the significance to them and their community. The teachers could also have a conversation about the procedures for obtaining permission to paint a mural on town property.

In the following geometry example, a teacher has created a task that uses skills and knowledge students have acquired over the course of a lesson, as well as integrating insight the teacher has gained about the students and community during that time, resulting in an exercise that exemplifies the culmination phase of the three-part lesson.

CCSS.MATH.CONTENT.HSG.MG.A.1

Use geometric shapes, their measures, and their properties to describe objects (e.g., modeling a tree trunk or a human torso as a cylinder).

CCSS.MATH.CONTENT.HSG.MG.A.2

Apply concepts of density based on area and volume in modeling situations (e.g., persons per square mile, BTUs per cubic foot).

CRMTask: How much shade is in your community?

Take a walk in your neighborhood. How many trees do you notice? How much shade are they providing? Estimate the area of shade for up to 5 of the trees you notice.

The teacher started by showing her students the *Involved* video on www.neighborhoodforest.org. The class then had a discussion about the benefits of trees for the environment, such as purifying the air, providing oxygen, and shade from the sun, as well as whether any of them had ever planted a tree. After discussing the abundance or lack of trees in their community, the teacher asked the students to select one of the trees on a street in their neighborhood to share the estimated area covered by the leaves. For the culmination, the class could engage in a cross-curricular activity where they take a closer look at the amount of air pollution that is blocked by an area with trees compared to an area that has fewer to no trees. For instance, students could analyze data sets similar to the one provided by Bennett and Turner (2020), where nitrogen dioxide diffusion tube readings from several streets over a year's time are compared to determine air pollution trends at certain times of year, whether or not an area is in close proximity to the roadside, and the type of road. The goal here is to highlight the mathematics in students' communities and to provide an opportunity for students to recognize not only the beauty of nature in their community but also how trees serve a dual purpose of helping reduce air pollution.

We have found that the culmination stage of lesson planning is a great time for teacher reflection and self-assessment, as well as a space when they can redirect the lesson if there is a disconnect between the cultural context and the mathematical context. Teachers can ask themselves these questions: Is the prompt strong enough by itself? Do I need to ask a question in the next phase? How is culture useful here? How do I connect this aspect of culture to this mathematical idea and possibly future mathematical ideas? What more do we have to learn about this particular cultural activity? Here, ways of knowing can be honored in similar ways as were identified in the launch, creating an opportunity to reconnect or connect the mathematical activity back to cultural knowledge and inquiry, particularly if opportunities have been missed earlier.

The culmination session is a place to look for climaxes, where student understanding of new mathematical cultural ideas comes to a shared point of understanding. An example might be the moment when students, having used multiple strategies to analyze the prices of houses between differently zoned neighborhoods, collectively begin to connect such price growth with ideas on gentrification. The teacher laid the foundation and asked the right probing questions to lead the students to organically arrive at an understanding of how math relates to social justice issues in their community.

CULTURALLY RELEVANT
MATHEMATICS CURRICULUM UNIT

As with any new strategy, one must have practice. Teachers can start that practice by revising existing math tasks to be more culturally relevant. They can then move on from thinking about a task to thinking about an entire lesson, during which they must think through the beginning (launch), middle (explore), and end (congress) of the lesson. Traditionally, we know that any lesson must begin with a goal, mathematics standards, lesson objectives, cognitively challenging mathematics tasks, and assessment procedures. In addition, teachers must also plan by providing a list of materials, anticipate student solution strategies, propose ways to address misconceptions, think of questions to elicit student thinking, orchestrate classroom discourse so that students make sense of the mathematics, and decide on instructional strategies that balance students' procedural and conceptual understanding of the mathematics. In our lesson plan template for culturally relevant mathematics, we refocus teacher thinking to begin with a goal that is centered in cultural and community knowledge.

When moving onto the next step of writing entire units, teachers are tasked with zooming out and looking at a larger picture than a single task or lesson. They must use knowledge of their students and community and decide on a larger social justice goal to unpack for a unit. In doing this, they learn that just as cognitive demand varies throughout a unit, so does cultural relevance. Although the unit's larger goal may have a social justice focus, teachers should also be aware that the objectives for each lesson will vary in the level of cultural relevance. Some lessons might be focused more on a mathematics objective, others might focus more on community values, and still others might be more balanced with mathematics shining the light on a community/cultural value. In the end, the unit should answer the question of how students will experience agency by using mathematics as a tool to understand and act on an issue that is important to them individually or collectively in their community or in the world.

The Food Deserts unit is an example of an exercise given to graduate in-service teachers. They were asked to design a culturally relevant mathematics unit either from scratch or modified from an existing unit in their curriculum. The teachers provided a summary of their unit, a description of each lesson in the unit, and the unit assessment. By having students investigate social issues that are highlighted in local/national/global news stories, they can learn how to apply important mathematics they've learned to generate solutions to these issues that are meaningful to them.

Mrs. LeMaire wants her students to have a better understanding of food insecurity. Many of them may have experienced it themselves as they attend a school in an area close to a food desert where many of the residents may experience food insecurity. The teacher wrote the following unit for her middle school students.

FOOD DESERTS: UNDERSTANDING FOOD JUSTICE USING A MATHEMATICAL LENS

Unit Overview: Students will work in groups to research the USDA definition, the causes, and the consequences of food deserts. They will notice and wonder about their findings as they relate to food insecurity based on race, ethnicity, and class. Students will explore their findings using a mathematical lens and will use mathematics to design solutions for the residents of food deserts.

Middle School Mathematics Content and Practice Standards:

CCSS.MATH.CONTENT.6.SP.B.4

Display numerical data in plots on a number line, including dot plots, histograms, and box plots.

CCSS.MATH.CONTENT.6.SP.B.5

Summarize numerical data sets in relation to their context.

CCSS.MATH.CONTENT.7.NS.A.3

Solve real-world and mathematical problems involving the four operations with rational numbers.

CCSS.MATH.CONTENT.7.G.B.4

Know the formulas for the area and circumference of a circle and use them to solve problems; give an informal derivation of the relationship between the circumference and area of a circle.

CCSS.MATH.CONTENT.7.EE.B.3

Solve real-life and mathematical problems using numerical and algebraic expressions and equations.

CCSS.MATH.PRACTICE.MP3 Construct viable arguments and critique the reasoning of others.

CCSS.MATH.PRACTICE.MP4 Model with mathematics.

CCSS.MATH.PRACTICE.MP5 Use appropriate tools strategically.

Lesson 1: Students will research what factors make a food desert according to the USDA. They can use USDA website resources such as www.ers.usda.gov/data-products/food-access-research-atlas/documentation *and* www.ers.usda.gov/publications/

pub-details/?pubid=42729 and print resources listed in the readings section. Students will mathematize the definition of a food desert using math equations with appropriate variables.

For homework (or in class), students will conduct an assessment of their local community to determine the types of and proximity of food retailers in their community. They will complete a checklist similar to the one shown here. The checklist will include food stores within a 2- to 3-mile radius from their home if they live in an urban setting, within 5 miles in a suburban area, and within 10 miles if they live in a rural area. Students can gather this data using an internet search if they are unable to travel to the stores.

NAME OF STORE	TYPE OF FOOD RETAILER: GROCERY, CONVENIENCE, FAST FOOD RESTAURANT	DISTANCE FROM HOME	SELLS FRESH FRUIT, VEGETABLES & OTHER HEALTHY FOOD OPTIONS

Lesson 2: Students will explore the relative cost of foods in their neighborhood and perform cost comparisons. First, they will discuss what they believe is a healthy diet. They will make a list of healthy food options that are staples for breakfast, lunch, and dinner. Students may use the Department of Agriculture's "Thrifty Food Plan" to help them plan a week's menu for a family of four. They will devise a menu and check the prices at two different stores in their neighborhood and determine which store in the neighborhood has more affordable prices for nutritious foods.

Lesson 3: Students will discuss whether or not they live in a food desert and how they know using mathematics. They will discuss if they live in an urban, rural, or suburban community. Are food deserts more prevalent in urban, rural, or suburban areas? Why? They will discuss the impact of living in a food desert. How does living in a food desert affect the residents? Some of the information will come from their research on food deserts. Using an online food desert tracker (such as the Food Access Research Atlas tool at www.ers.usda.gov), students will find the closest food desert to their school (or home) if they live more than a few miles from the school. They will explore other areas (in their state or areas of interest across the nation) where there are food deserts. What do they notice? What questions do they have?

Lesson 4: Based on their research about food deserts, students will come up with a problem they want to explore. They will clarify what the problem is and decide on a question they can collect data on. They will design and implement a plan to collect data. For homework (or next class), students will collect data appropriate to their question.

Lesson 5: Students will create a graphical or tabular display for their data. They will analyze the data and discuss it with their group. For homework (or next class), students will write a brief report of the problem, questions, data display, analysis, conclusions, and next steps.

Lesson 6: Student presentations: Students will report on their data in reference to what they learned about food deserts in their town/city. They might address such topics as limited access to affordable fresh fruit and vegetables and other healthy foods, food insecurity, economic and health disparities, and causes of food deserts and possible solutions.

Assessment: This is a great place to have students focus on social action. Remember the social justice standards in Chapter 6. The Social Justice Anchor Standard 13 states that "students will analyze the harmful impact of bias and injustice on the world, historically and today." In Lessons 4–6, students should have learned about the problems and effects of living in a food desert. The goal of the assessment is for them to synthesize this information and research possible solutions. Students are being asked to mathematize the problem of where to place an affordable fresh food resource for the community living in a food desert. They should also recognize the food injustice that people experience solely on the basis of their zip code.

Students will design a solution to help their community or another community that is a food desert. What can residents do to remedy the low access to healthy foods in their neighborhood? Determine where a fresh food resource such as a grocery store, supermarket, farmer's market, or community garden is needed and then answer this question: How can we use mathematics to assist the residents in making a convincing argument for getting a fresh food resource in the community? This is one example of a question that could be answered during the assessment phase. Students may have come up with other questions as well. Students will be required to model their solution using geometric measures of center or other grade-level appropriate mathematics. For example, students might present a drawing of the supermarket as the center of a circle and a 2- to 3-mile radius (for an urban area; 5-mile radius for a suburban area; and 10-mile radius for a rural area) drawn to show the area with easy access to nutritious foods. The final assessment is a clearly stated solution plan for the residents.

Readings for Unit on Food Deserts:

1. Characteristics and Influential Factors of Food Deserts, 2012

2. The Grocery Gap: Who Has Access to Healthy Food and Why It Matters, Sarah Treuhaft – PolicyLink & Allison Karpyn – The Food Trust, 2010

3. USDA Report to Congress, 2009. Access to Affordable and Nutritious Food: Measuring and Understanding Food Deserts and Their Consequences

A similar unit may be designed for high school students based on the following standards:

High School Mathematics Content and Practice Standards:
CCSS.MATH.CONTENT.HSG.MG.A.1
Use geometric shapes, their measures, and their properties to describe objects (e.g., modeling a tree trunk or a human torso as a cylinder).
CCSS.MATH.CONTENT.HSG.MG.A.2
Apply concepts of density based on area and volume in modeling situations (e.g., persons per square mile, BTUs per cubic foot).
CCSS.MATH.CONTENT.HSG.MG.A.3
Apply geometric methods to solve design problems (e.g., designing an object or structure to satisfy physical constraints or minimize cost; working with typographic grid systems based on ratios).
CCSS.MATH.PRACTICE.MP3 Construct viable arguments and critique the reasoning of others.
CCSS.MATH.PRACTICE.MP4 Model with mathematics.

Source: Adapted from Madura & McDermott (2022).

In creating this unit, the teacher, Mrs. LeMaire, used several of the strategies we've shared throughout this book. She thought about how to make a real-world connection between the mathematics of the unit and her students. The neighborhood where the school is located is considered a food desert, which is an area that has limited access to affordable and nutritious food. Although there are seasonal pop-up farmer's markets in the city, they are usually not within walking distance of this neighborhood. For this reason, Mrs. LeMaire decided to focus on having the students learn about how they could help their community overcome the effects of living in a food desert. By doing this, Mrs. LeMaire is planning a unit that places community knowledge front and center. While every lesson involves mathematics to some degree, some lessons are focused more on the mathematics, while others are focused on students learning about several social aspects of their community. It is important for students to know the history of their community and the possibilities of a brighter future for the community. For example, one student group researched their city for open areas where they could create community gardens.

We believe that action is a necessary step in building agency for students. This agency can be nurtured by inviting the students to discuss their solution idea and decide on the best way for collective action in creating a community garden. This would also be a great place to involve parents, families, and the community. A missed opportunity in the unit is not involving the community and families in the first place. Having students research information about their community/town is great; however, seeking knowledge directly from community influencers/elders can yield authentic information that will help students to see the real-world connections of the math they are doing. Students can also see how they can use mathematics to change something that is problematic into something that can bring the community more joy and healthy living.

Looking back at Figure 5.2 Approaching Cultural Inquiry From a "We" Perspective, we can see that this unit really does address the idea of We Respond, especially if the students get their families and community involved in the community garden. By including the community in the planning of the garden, students will recognize that something they learn in school can model "care, love, and respect" for their community. The closure should include a product that points back at the big idea, which is learning something about the community and taking action, using mathematics as a tool.

The flow of this unit started with a big idea (food injustice). Once the teacher had her big idea in mind, she thought about possible resources to align her idea to grade-level math content standards. The idea of researching food deserts has many opportunities for mathematics connections. In particular, the seventh-grade standards listed are part of her school's mathematics curriculum. Appropriate timing plays a part in building a unit, so Mrs. LeMaire thought about individual lessons where subsequent lessons would build on previous lessons, making sure to have just enough content for students' deep learning of the mathematics.

IMPROVE

Choose one of the lessons from the Food Desert unit and discuss how the Launch–Explore–Culminate process might play out in the classroom.

Teachers can be successful when they are provided the tools and opportunities to create culturally relevant mathematics tasks, lessons, and units. The process of learning about and creating CRMTasks is an ongoing process—a journey that you will take throughout your entire teaching career. Task creation is just one aspect that we hope you feel confident in tackling at this point, which includes skills you can apply to all aspects of designing culturally relevant lessons and units.

Summary and Discussion Questions

This chapter further explored culturally relevant math tasks by introducing the Revising a Math Task to Be Culturally Relevant Template. We then brought together what we have discussed regarding CRMTasks in past chapters to implement in a lesson plan, using the three-part lesson format Launch–Explore–Culminate/Congress. In the launch we presented in this chapter, the "lean in" came from a personal experience for the teacher, which is just one of many ways to engage authentically with one's classroom. A key component of the launch is the environment in which students are engaged in risk-taking, collaboration, and knowledge construction, where the teacher and student become co-creators of context and content. In the explore phase, students utilize various strategies, communication, and tools to engage in the tasks. In this part of the lesson, teachers learn about student understandings and misunderstandings and together determine an answer to the question, Why is this problem strategy important to *us*? Finally, in the culmination/congress phase, the teacher facilitates active discourse during which students can make sense of and refine their ideas, creating space for students to share co-creations, strategies, feelings, empathy, and responses to action. This approach to lesson planning is invaluable in planning whole curriculum units, as illustrated in the example culturally relevant mathematics curriculum unit included in this chapter.

For the following questions, consider a task or lesson that you have been working on and think through the following questions as you create powerful experiences:

1. Are there "culturally neutral" concepts that you can replace with a more culturally relevant and community-minded idea? How might you then "lean in" to launch your lesson?
2. In the explore phase, think of how you can deliberately attend to notions of cultural ways of knowing, affirmation, celebration, and solidarity. Give a few examples.
3. In the culminate/congress phase, can you think of a time when knowledge of your students' community helped redirect or bring back the cultural context during a mathematics task? What was the disconnect with the original mathematical context? What questions do you think are helpful to guide this redirecting or reconnection?

CHAPTER 9

Continuing the Journey

In this chapter, we will

1. Summarize key elements for designing culturally relevant mathematics tasks
2. Highlight critical areas for the development of teachers for creating culturally relevant mathematics tasks

Becoming proficient at creating tasks for culturally relevant mathematics teaching is just the beginning of a lifelong journey for a teacher. There will likely be starts and stops, as well as successful and challenging moments. Now, we will look back on the earlier work in this book to reflect on key points and give our last advice on handling the day-to-day challenges of continuing this journey.

REFLECTING ON KEY ELEMENTS

In Chapter 1, we explored expectations for modern mathematics and fundamental ideas about culturally relevant teaching to begin the journey to engage children in culturally relevant mathematics teaching. We raise several suppositions for teaching mathematics:

- Students deserve access to mathematical challenge, desire, thriving, and promise as a baseline—not a ceiling.
- Who students are—that is, their culture and community—is central to their mathematical identities and experiences.
- Children thrive when mathematics experiences shape their lives and empower them to respond with empathy and agency.

We also framed three important tenets of culturally relevant mathematics teaching:

1. Offer challenging mathematics experiences where students have access and are engaged as doers and creators of mathematics.
2. Create mathematics contexts, prompts, and inquiries that build from cultural and community sources.
3. Provide intentional task outcomes for hope, empathy, and critical agency as students practice mathematics.

In Chapter 2, we introduced you to Culturally Relevant Mathematics Practices, which paint a picture of mathematics learning where learners thrive and find voice and meaning in the mathematics that they do. We expanded the definition of a task to include cultural context and social prompts and explored features of culturally relevant, cognitively demanding tasks.

In Chapter 3, we identified three task-building actions for culturally relevant mathematics tasks that were framed as the key work in making culturally relevant math practices a reality for children. These actions form the heart of design work: establishing demand (Demand); centering community and cultural inquiry (Relevance); and targeting empathy, agency, and action (Agency; see Figure 3.1). We also introduced the CRCD mathematics task rubric to support how the dimensions of demand, agency, and relevance can be assessed by teachers as emerging, developing, or exemplary (see Figure 3.3).

In Chapters 4, 5, and 6, we described and illustrated 12 specific approaches for planning and designing CRMTasks (Figure 9.1). The process involves planning with intentional goals for creating hope and centering relevance and agency. The process also involves attending to students' culture and community using our We Care/We Belong approach, which is essential to nurture authentic relationships with your students. In addition to accomplishing this through your daily interactions, teachers can conduct a student interview, create contexts using cultural artifacts, or take a Community Walk to determine funds of knowledge in your school's community. We shared some strategies for creating context of supporting community aspirations and creating prompts in solidarity with emerging social and racial justice issues.

In Chapter 7, we shared our work and lessons learned from how teachers view culturally relevant teaching, as well as tools we and others have created along the way. In Chapter 8, we discussed how you might frame a powerful teaching approach called teaching through problem-solving through the lens of culturally relevant pedagogy (launch–explore–culminate/congress). Finally, we shared a template for revising existing tasks to be more culturally relevant and included an example of how one can integrate CRMTasks in lessons and curriculum units.

FIGURE 9.1 ● Twelve specific approaches for planning and designing CRMTasks

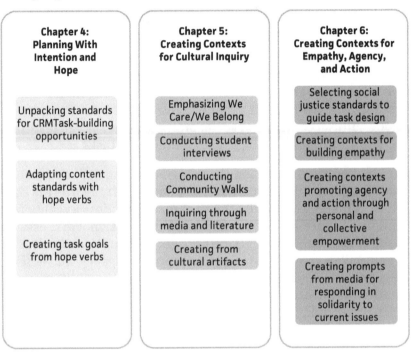

Chapter 4: Planning With Intention and Hope	Chapter 5: Creating Contexts for Cultural Inquiry	Chapter 6: Creating Contexts for Empathy, Agency, and Action
Unpacking standards for CRMTask-building opportunities	Emphasizing We Care/We Belong	Selecting social justice standards to guide task design
Adapting content standards with hope verbs	Conducting student interviews	Creating contexts for building empathy
Creating task goals from hope verbs	Conducting Community Walks	Creating contexts promoting agency and action through personal and collective empowerment
	Inquiring through media and literature	
	Creating from cultural artifacts	Creating prompts from media for responding in solidarity to current issues

KEYS TO CONTINUING THE JOURNEY: HOPE BY DESIGN

We started off by saying that we see teachers as engineers, and we would like to emphasize that again. Teachers are engineers capable of designing—and refining—engaging, inspiring, and empowering mathematics learning experiences for their students.

So how can we continue the work of culturally relevant teaching and the design of culturally relevant mathematics tasks? Teachers are challenged at every phase of the work of design, whether it's planning, creating, improving, or implementing. Throughout the book, we have sought to engage the reader with engineering verbs to aid in developing a design mindset: ask, imagine, plan, create, and improve. Furthermore, we extended the conversation to talk about what happens when teachers continue on a journey in which they will have to continually ask, imagine, plan, and create an improved mathematics task for the children they teach. It is helpful to get in a proactive mindset, anticipating what issues and problems might arise, and using the tools and skills at your disposal to respond skillfully.

ONE TASK AT A TIME

Sometimes when people start this journey, they want to look at entire units and lessons. That's fine, but the truth of the matter is that it is often more manageable to take it one task at a time, one question at a time, one problem at a time, one prompt at a time, one context at a time—that is, it's okay to start small. In fact, it is often wise to start with reasonable goals and build up from there, especially if this is all new to you or you are just starting out. We are constantly amazed at how one task—just one task—causes us to think deeply about things like cognitive demand, the power of cultural inquiry, or the extent of critical consciousness. In each task, there exists a world of possibilities.

OPEN UP YOUR PRACTICE

When you begin to teach in a way that uses tasks that students might find interesting or engaging, the classroom and extended community changes, whether these are tasks that they create themselves or tasks that you create in collaboration with them. One of the telltale signs of success will be the way in which they begin to discuss these experiences. Open up your practice to feedback from students directly and from community members at large. When you invite feedback and hear it with genuine care and consideration, people will be more willing to discuss and talk about things that relate to them and that are relatable to them. Some of the examples included in our book have been based on the feedback we have received from students and from their teachers. This feedback can range from topics that are critical to them to their definitions of culturally relevant teaching or culturally relevant mathematics. It's important because it helps us to adjust how we are implementing and creating tasks so we can ensure we are doing so with the utmost respect for the communities we serve.

JUMP IN AT THE DEEP END

Something that continues to come up in our practice and in our everyday lives is that it is impossible to do this work without centering and immersing oneself into the culture and community of the people one teaches. The obvious reason is that by doing this, you will continue to build a treasure trove of cultural knowledge. However, the most important reason is that you develop a symbiosis with the community that you're seeking to understand through deep relationships. It is through the presence of authentic relationships that the design process we've outlined, particularly the imagining, is most profoundly expressed. When we are connected with our students, we are able to see what they see. We can imagine contexts *for* and *with* them to drive our mathematics. In doing so, we are also more open to the contexts they create and imagine. We become more trusting of the mathematics embedded in their culture and community, and we build an empathetic relationship with those communities.

PREPARE TO ENGAGE STUDENTS IN SOCIAL JUSTICE

The main places where teachers get stuck when designing culturally relevant math tasks are understanding where the issues come from and discerning what might be appropriate for students to learn. Adolescents and teenagers deserve to learn mathematics in ways that shape their lives and the lives of those around them. But we acknowledge that engaging young people can be a source of unease for some teachers. Before beginning to engage in social justice work, we see at least four key checks to carry out with students:

1. Start with familiar topics.
2. Scan community organizations.
3. Ensure parent and school permissions.
4. Check personal bias and deficit mindsets.

Think about it. Adolescents learn pretty early that math experiences can be playful on one hand, where games are played, marbles are counted, pizza is divided, and candies given away. This often results in trivial problem sets and word problems that make no real sense (e.g., Fran purchases 21 chocolate bars. If Fran gives away 6, how many does she have?). One way to begin to engage is to use familiar topics and approaches and then gradually "problematize" the context and prompt to shift toward challenges of fairness, equity, and justice. We also suggest that you perform a community pulse check to gain better awareness of school and parental consent for pursuing justice topics. Communities have ready-made aspirations for justice work, and it often means tapping into local change networks—nonprofits, government agencies, churches, social groups, and the like. You are not alone, nor solely responsible for "bringing justice."

We see so many teachers struggle in isolation with ethical questions and their discomfort in having these difficult—and necessary—conversations. We prioritize this for mathematics teaching because of the imbalance in racing toward the end goal of abstract math tasks ("naked math," as we call it, or those with "neutral" math contexts) for young learners. Our advice is to get support from existing curricula and standards guides and the various organizations that have developed guidance for having social justice conversations.

It is also important not to forget the roles parents and community have played in our work around CRMTasks. Parents also play an important part in considering what they want their children to learn and do in school. Understanding how parents feel about current issues and what they see as critical, and challenging, topics and issues to learn is crucial. We hope that you see mathematics teaching as a partnership where parents and community can inform—even guide—what is important to explore, respond to, and challenge.

Although not altogether the focus of this book, we acknowledge that far too many teachers approach thinking about culture, justice, and community in deficit ways—that is, as teachers, we often place ourselves outside of communities and see our work as fixing something deficient. We also believe that all teachers hold potentially damaging biases (e.g., believing rap music is a default way to engage Black children). These biases must be checked openly in the planning and reflecting process.

ROUND AND ROUND: SEE CULTURALLY RELEVANT PEDAGOGY AS CIRCULAR

Our definitions and frameworks—the ways in which we interpret and apply CRP—continue to evolve. Take, for example, our guide for creating cultural mathematics tasks (Figure 3.1). There is an almost linear feel to it: Demand Relevance Agency. One teacher interpreted this as "I need to start on Demand and end up with Agency." However, as we grow, we continue to think about culturally relevant mathematics teaching as a nonlinear process where the elements of Demand, Relevance, and Agency work together in ways that sometimes make it difficult to distinguish between them.

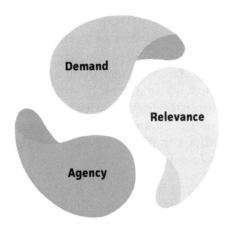

While we do believe that high cognitive demand ought to be a baseline indicator of work in CRMTasks, it is rare that we see tasks that are strong in every dimension. For instance, there are situations where current events and pressing issues of racial injustice may provide an opportunity for creating a task; the improvement work needed may be to strengthen the math demand substantially. This might be considered an Emerging task (see our rubric, Figure 3.3). The same may be true with tasks that begin in an interesting pursuit of cultural inquiry but which may require improvement in both Demand and Agency. Some tasks may have strong elements of cognitive demand as well as cultural inquiry but may lack a context or prompt that allows students to experience critical agency. While there is a tendency to see the latter example as Exemplary, the omission of agency is harmful to the overall work for CRP. When we think about CRMTasks in this way, our advice to teachers is to start where you are comfortable and work from your strengths to improve and refine the other elements of the task. What matters most is that you are approaching this important—and often difficult—work with a spirit of caring, curiosity, empathy, and open-mindedness.

Above all else: Embrace the journey.

Summary and Discussion Questions

You have been on a journey with us throughout this book, digging deeper into culturally relevant mathematics teaching and culturally relevant mathematics practices to build culturally relevant mathematics tasks that will enhance your lessons, instruction, and your students' experience with mathematics. It's a lot of information to take in, and we encourage you to look back at the book often to reacquaint yourself with the tools and insights offered here. As you reflect on all you have learned, consider the following questions:

1. Describe some ways in which your understandings about teaching math and engaging communities have shifted since engaging in the activities and questions throughout this book.
2. Where do you rate yourself on the journey to fully utilize culturally relevant mathematics teaching and tasks as a part of your teaching? What do you see as strengths? Where might you grow?
3. What possibilities of fostering hope in the mathematics experiences of students do you see? How can you build and grow a movement of teaching change that draws upon hope as a source of mathematics teaching where you are? Describe what critical next steps you see in your development as a practitioner of culturally relevant mathematics teaching.
4. What are some plans you can make for the future to further expand the critical-, cultural-, and community-mindedness of your teaching?

Resources

1. The Southern Poverty Law Center's website, *Learning for Justice* (www.splcenter.org/learning-for-justice), provides excellent guidance on several topic areas such as race and ethnicity, religion, ability, class, immigration, gender and sexual identity, bullying and bias, and rights and activism.

2. Resources for including diverse mathematicians in math tasks/lessons/units:
   a. *Mathematically Gifted & Black* (www.mathematicallygiftedandblack.com)
   b. *Lathisms* (www.lathisms.org)
   c. About Us—*Indigenous Mathematicians* (indigenousmathematicians.org/about-us)
   d. *Mathematicians of the African Diaspora* (www.mathad.com/home)
   e. *Meet a Mathematician*—(www.meetamathematician.com and various videos on YouTube)

3. *Rethinking Schools*—Bringing more critical voices into the conversation about public schools and libraries (www.rethinkingschools.org)

4. Resources for more information about the Ishango bone
   a. *Mathematical Association of America: Mathematical Treasure: Ishango Bone* (www.maa.org/press/periodicals/convergence/mathematical-treasure-ishango-bone)
   b. *Mathematicians of the African Diaspora: An Old Mathematical Object* (the Ishango bone) (math.buffalo.edu/mad/AncientAfrica/ishango)

5. Selected youth literature

NO.	BOOK TITLE	AUTHOR
1	*A Soft Place to Land*	Janae Marks
2	*Ancestor Approved: Intertribal Stories for Kids*	Cynthia Leitich Smith
3	*Building Zaha: The Story of Architect Zaha Hadid*	Victoria Tentler-Krylov
4	*Home Is Not a Country*	Sofia Elhillo

NO.	BOOK TITLE	AUTHOR
5	*Maya and the Robot*	Eve L. Ewing, Illustrated by Christine Almeda
6	*On the Come Up*	Angie Thomas
7	*One Crazy Summer*	Rita Williams-Garcia
8	*Take Back the Block*	Chrystal Giles
9	*The Compton Cowboys: And the Fight to Save Their Horse Ranch, Young Readers' Edition*	Walter Thompson-Hernández
10	*Women Who Count: Honoring African American Women Mathematicians*	Shelly M. Jones

Appendix A: Revising a Math Task to Be Culturally Relevant Template

Goal: Describe the current state of your task and your desired movement on the CRCD mathematics task rubric (Emerging to Developing to Exemplary).	
Original task (Should be a cognitively demanding task)	Math content/standards
Why did you choose this task? What aspect of the task was the focus? (Mirror/window, community knowledge, social justice, math content is CR friendly, etc.)	
Using the CRCD mathematics task rubric, describe how the math task was revised.	
Revised CRMTask	How will this empower students?

Appendix B: Culturally Relevant Teaching Lesson Plan Template

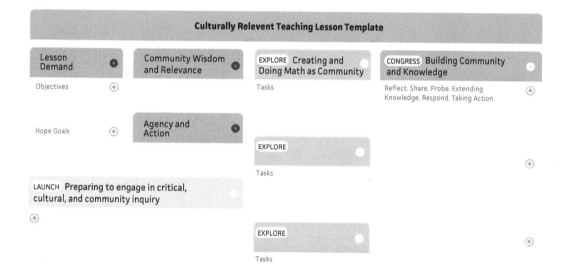

Appendix C: List of Tasks and Math Content Standard With Grade

CCSS	PROBLEM CONTEXT AND MATH CONTENT	PAGE
7.RP.A.3	Percentage change in population of Austin, Texas	4
HSA.APR.C.5	Vignette 1: Mr. Ira teaching multiplying binomials	5
7.RP.A.2.C	Version A: Solve the proportion math task	6
7.RP.A.2.C	Version B: Solve the salary problem using a proportion	6
7.RP.A.2	Vignette 2: Mrs. Herrington addresses homelessness in the community task	11
6.NS.B.3	Vignette 3: Mr. Canton's lesson on resourcefulness during the pandemic—using decimal operations in a recipe for hand sanitizer	12
HSG.MG.A.2	Vignette 4: Mr. Aizawa's students apply concepts of density to explore health disparities in a rural school district	17
HSN.VM.A.3	Figure 2.1: Sample Structure of a Mathematics Task—Velocity	22
7.SP.C.5	Figure 2.2: Sample Structure of a Mathematics Task—Probability	22
HSN.Q.A.3	Vignette 5: #Muslim: Building student identity with Islamic tessellations	25
6.G.A.1	Vignette 6: Mr. Eaton's sixth graders use area, surface area, and volume to design a TikTok video backdrop	26
8.G.C.9	Taking walks during the pandemic, noticing 3D figures, and using volume formulas to model those figures	28
6.SP.B.5.C	Vignette 7: Ms. Alvarez's lesson on exploring the link between asthma and poor air quality using measures of center	29

(continued)

(continued)

CCSS	PROBLEM CONTEXT AND MATH CONTENT	PAGE
HSG.SRT.A.2	Using scale factor to determine the size of a two-car garage	77
HSF.LE.A.1.C	How fast is the algae growing in a local pond?	78
7.NS.1, 7.NS.3	Modeling human innovation over time using negative and positive integers on a number line	80
6.NS.B.4	Mr. Frazer's sixth-grade class explores the cost of a family reunion	81
	Vignette 10: Getting to know a student different than me	84
	Vignette 11: Getting to know a student: Faster isn't smarter	85
	Vignette 12: Community Walk: Getting to know the town where students live	89
	Vignette 13: Community Walk: Neighborhood market versus supermarket	90
6.EE.C.9	Mr. Cook's class investigates the contributions of Chinese immigrants to the transcontinental railroad and the payments they received using a given formula	102
8.SP.A.1	What factors influence homelessness: Interpreting a line of best fit	103
HSG.MG.A.2	Exploring gentrification through the concept of population density	105
6.G.A.4 7.G.B.6	Using surface area to assist in a neighborhood cleanup	106
7.NS.A.3	Making the case to add internet towers to underresourced neighborhoods	108
HSG.GMD.A.3	Shingle Mountain: Tackling a recycling problem using a volume formula for cylinders	110
6.EE.A.2, 6.EE.A.3, 6.EE.A.4	Creating equivalent expressions using an Islamic tessellation pattern	128
HSF.IF.B.4	Students interpret functions related to community inquiry about neighborhood grocery stores	132
HSG.MG.A.1	Using geometric measure to create murals of social movements	138
HSG.MG.A.2	How much shade is in your community? Students use the concept of density to explore	139

CCSS	PROBLEM CONTEXT AND MATH CONTENT	PAGE
6.SP.B.4, 6.SP.B.5 7.NS.A.3 7.GB.4 7.EE.B.3	Middle school food desert curriculum unit	142
HSG.MG.A.1, HSG.MG.A.2, HSG.MG.A.3	High school food desert curriculum unit	145

References

Aguirre, J., Mayfield-Ingram, K., & Martin, D. B. (2013). *The impact of identity in K–5 mathematics: Rethinking equity-based practices.* National Council of Teachers of Mathematics.

Aguirre, J. M., & Zavala, M. del R. (2013). Making culturally responsive mathematics teaching explicit: A lesson analysis tool. *Pedagogies: An International Journal,* 8(2),163–190.

Bennett, H., & Turner, K. (2020). *How do trees clean our air?* https://edu.rsc.org/feature/how-do-trees-clean-our-air/4010864.article

Berry, R. Q., Conway, B. M., Lawler, B. R., & Staley, J. W. (2020). *High school mathematics lessons to explore, understand, and respond to social injustice.* Corwin.

Civil, M., & Andrade, R. (2003). Collaborative practice with parents: The role of the researcher as mediator. In A. Peter-Koop (Ed.), *Collaboration in teacher education: Examples from the context of mathematics education* (Vol. 1, pp. 153–168). Kluwer Academic.

Coogler, R. (2018). *Black Panther.* Walt Disney Studios Motion Pictures.

Enyedy, N., & Mukhopadhyay, S. (2007). They don't show nothing I didn't know: Emergent tensions between culturally relevant pedagogy and mathematics pedagogy. *Journal of the Learning Sciences, 16*(2), 139–174.

Fears, D. (2020, November 16). Shingle mountain: How a pile of toxic pollution was dumped in a community of color. *Washington Post.* https://www.washingtonpost.com/climate-environment/2020/11/16/environmentalracism-dallas-shingle-mountain/

Foote, M. Q., Roth McDuffie, A., Aguirre, J., Turner, E. E., Drake, C., & Bartell, T. G. (2015). Mathematics learning case study module. In C. Drake et al. (Eds.), *TeachMath learning modules for K–8 mathematics methods courses: Teachers empowered to advance change in mathematics project.* https:www.teachmath.info

Ghiles, C. (2021). *Take back the block.* Random House for Young Readers.

Godin, T. L. (2017). *Hula-hoopin queen* (V. Brantley-Newton, Illus.). Lee & Low Books.

Gutierrez, R. (2016). Strategies for creative insubordination in mathematics teaching. *Teaching for Excellence and Equity in Mathematics, 7*(1), 52–60.

Gutstein, E., Lipman, P., Hernandez, P., & de los Reyes, R. (1997). Culturally relevant mathematics teaching in a Mexican American context. *Journal for Research in Mathematics Education, 28*(6), 709–737.

Gutstein, E., & Peterson, B. (2013). *Rethinking mathematics: Teaching social justice by the numbers.* Rethinking Schools.

Hammond, Z. (2014). *Culturally responsive teaching and the brain.* Corwin.

Jones, S. M. (2015). Mathematics teachers' use of the culturally relevant cognitively demanding task framework and rubric in the classroom. *NERA Conference Proceedings 2015.* https://opencommons.uconn.edu/nera-2015/12

Jones, S. M. (2018). Teachers' conceptions of teaching mathematics for social justice: Building on their knowledge of culturally relevant pedagogy. *New England Mathematics Journal, 51*(2), 50–63.

Jones, S. M., & Pearson, D. (2013). Music: Highly engaged students connect music to math. *General Music Today, 27*(1), 18–23. https://doi.org/10.1177/1048371313486478

Joseph, G. G. (2011). *The crest of the peacock: Non-European roots of mathematics* (3rd ed.). Princeton University Press.

Kennedy, L., Corriher, B., & Root, D. (2016, October 19). *Redistricting and representation.* Center for American Progress. https://www.americanprogress.org/article/redistricting-and-representation/

Khalil, A. (2020). *The Arabic quilt: An immigrant story* (A. Semirdzhyan, Illus.). Tilbury House.

Krull, K. (2003). *Harvesting hope: The story of Cesar Chavez* (Y. Morales, Illus.). Harcourt.

Ladson-Billings, G. (1994). *The dreamkeepers: Successful teachers of African-American children.* Jossey Bass.

Ladson-Billings, G. (1995). Toward a theory of culturally relevant pedagogy. *American Educational Research Journal, 35,* 465–491.

Ladson-Billings, G. (2009). *The dreamkeepers: Successful teachers of African-American children* (2nd ed.). Jossey Bass.

Leonard, J., & Guha, S. (2002). Creating cultural relevance in teaching and learning mathematics. *Teaching Children Mathematics, 9*(2), 114–118.

Madura, J., & McDermott, B. (2022). Hungry for change: Food deserts in CT. In K. Evans & M. Staples (Eds.), *Connecting mathematics and social justice: Lessons and resources for secondary math teachers.* Math Teachers' Circle 4 Social Justice.

Martinez, E. J. (2018). *Cuando amamos cantamos/When we love someone we sing to them* (B. Vidal, Illus.). Children's Book Press.

Matthews, L. E. (2003). Babies overboard! The complexities of incorporating culturally relevant teaching into mathematics instruction. *Educational Studies in Mathematics, 53,* 61–82.

Matthews, L. E. (2005). Toward design of clarifying equity messages in mathematics reform. *The High School Journal, 88*(4), 46–58.

Matthews, L. E. (2009). Identity crisis: The public stories of mathematics educators. *Journal of Urban Mathematics Education, 2*(1), 1–4.

Matthews, L. E. (2018). 2008—Illuminating urban excellence: A movement of change within mathematics education. *Journal of Urban Mathematics Education, 11,* 1–2.

Matthews, L. E., Jones, S. M., & Parker, Y. A. (2013). Advancing a framework of culturally relevant, cognitively demanding mathematics tasks. In J. Leonard & D. B. Martin (Eds.), *The brilliance of Black children in mathematics: Beyond the numbers and toward a new discourse* (pp. 123–150). Information Age.

Moore, M. A. (2020, Summer). The new reparations math. *UCONN Magazine.* https://magazine.uconn.edu/2020/06/15/the-new-reparations-math/#

National Council of Teachers of English. (2020, July 13). *Key aspects of critical literacy: An excerpt.* NCTE. https://ncte.org/blog/2019/07/critical-literacy/

National Council of Teachers of Mathematics. (2000). *Principles and standards for school mathematics.* NCTM.

National Council of Teachers of Mathematics. (2018). *Catalyzing change in high school mathematics: Initiating critical conversations.* NCTM.

National Council of Teachers of Mathematics. (2020). *Catalyzing change in middle school mathematics: Initiating critical conversations.* NCTM.

National Governors Association Center for Best Practices, Council of Chief State School Officers. (2010). *Common Core State Standards Mathematical Practice.* National Governors Association Center for Best Practices, Council of Chief State School Officers, Washington, D.C.

Newell, C. (2021). *If you lived during the Plimoth Thanksgiving* (W. Nelson, Illus.). Scholastic Press.

Schrock, C., Norris, K., Pugalee, D. K., Seitz, R., & Hollinghead, F. (2013). *NCSM great tasks for mathematics, 6–12*. National Council of Supervisors of Mathematics.

Shetterly, M. L. (2016). *Hidden figures: The American dream and the untold story of the Black women mathematicians who helped win the space race*. William Morrow.

Stein, M. K., Grover, B. W., & Henningsen, M. (1996). Building student capacity for mathematical thinking and reasoning: An analysis of mathematical tasks used in reform classrooms. *American Educational Research Journal, 33*(2), 455–488.

Stein, M. K., Smith, M. S., Henningsen, M. A., & Silver, E. A. (2000). *Implementing standards-based mathematics instruction: A casebook for professional development*. National Council of Teachers of Mathematics.

Tate, W. (2004). "Brown," political economy, and the scientific education of African Americans. *Review of Research in Education, 28*, 147–184.

Taylor, P. C. (1996). Mythmaking and mythbreaking in the mathematics classroom. *Educational Studies in Mathematics, 31*(1/2), 151–173. http://www.jstor.org/stable/3482938

Turner, E. E., & Strawhun, B. T. (2007). Posing problems that matter: Investigating school overcrowding. *Teaching Children Mathematics, 13*(9), 457–463.

United States Department of Agriculture. (2015, June). Food environment atlas. *USDA Economic Research Service*. http://www.ers.usda.gov/data-products/food-environment-atlas/about-the-atlas.apx

Wiggins, G., & McTighe, J. (2005). *Understanding by design*. Association for Supervision and Curriculum Development.

Zevenbergen, R. (1996). Constructivism as a liberal bourgeois discourse. *Educational Studies in Mathematics, 31*, 95–113.

Index

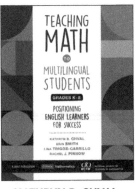
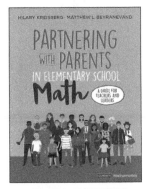

**JENNIFER M. BAY-WILLIAMS,
JOHN J. SANGIOVANNI, ROSALBA SERRANO,
SHERRI MARTINIE, JENNIFER SUH**

Because fluency is so much more
than basic facts and algorithms

Grades K–8

**KAREN S. KARP,
BARBARA J. DOUGHERTY,
SARAH B. BUSH**

A schoolwide solution for students'
mathematics success

Elementary, Middle School, High School

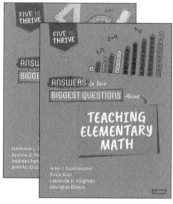

**JOHN J. SANGIOVANNI, SUSIE KATT,
LATRENDA D. KNIGHTEN, GEORGINA RIVERA,
FREDERICK L. DILLON, AYANNA D. PERRY,
ANDREA CHENG, JENNIFER OUTZS**

Actionable answers to your most
pressing questions about teaching
elementary and secondary math

Elementary, Secondary

**SARA DELANO MOORE,
KIMBERLY RIMBEY**

A journey toward making
manipulatives meaningful

Grades K–3, 4–8

CORWIN

A SAGE Publishing Company

Helping educators make the greatest impact

CORWIN HAS ONE MISSION: to enhance education through intentional professional learning.

We build long-term relationships with our authors, educators, clients, and associations who partner with us to develop and continuously improve the best evidence-based practices that establish and support lifelong learning.